By Philip Rapp

Edited by Ben Ohmart

The Baby Snook Scripts Volume 3
© 2018. The Philip Rapp Estate All rights reserved.

No part of this book may be reproduced in any form or by any means, electronic, mechanical, digital, photocopying or recording, except for the inclusion in a review, without permission in writing from the publisher.

Published in the USA by:
BearManor Media
P O Box 71426
Albany, Georgia 31708
www.bearmanormedia.com

Printed in the United States of America
IISBN   978-1-62933-259-8 (paperback)

Book design and layout by Darlene Swanson • www.van-garde.com

Table of Contents

1. The Pet Store...................................1
2. A Night Snack..................................9
3. Daddy Invents Water (January 18, 1940)..................17
4. Baseball (June 15, 1939)..........................49
5. New Baby (June 22, 1939)..........................63
6. Snooks at the Museum (for TV, April 17, 1949).............73
7. Playing Hooky (April 13, 1939)......................89
8. Daddy Buys Snooks a Stove (April 20, 1939)...............99
9. At the Dentist................................111
10. Golfing....................................119
11. At the Hospital (May 25, 1939).....................133
12. Butterfly...................................141
13. Elopement (story treatment).......................149
14. Painting (full script of Good News of 1939,
    September 29, 1938)............................151
15. Insomnia (full script of Maxwell House Coffee Time,
    October 1, 1942)..............................197

16.	Homework (February 15, 1940)	229
17.	The Newspaper (March 7, 1940)	241
18.	Plane Flight (March 14, 1940)	255
19.	Snooks Steals a Tooth (March 28, 1940)	269
20.	The Phone Bill (April 4, 1940)	281
21.	At the Movies (April 11, 1940)	295
22.	Magician (April 18, 1940)	309
23.	Partial Notes and Script for a Baby Snooks Show	323
24.	C Note (story treatment)	329
25.	Thanksgiving	331
26.	Treasure (story treatment)	337
27.	Telling Time	339
28.	Snooks Synopses (story ideas)	345

Foreword

Welcome, gang, to the third edition of Baby Snooks Scripts!

Let the applause herald Frank Morgan, Meredith Willson, Hanley Stafford, and Fanny Brice in rompers as the one and only… Baby Snooks!

You might notice some strange things in this edition. These scripts are from a variety of times and typewriters, but as a completest myself, I like to keep things as close to how they were originally written as possible, to show you just how the scripts really were back then. That's why you might notice some formatting differences between scripts, non-uniformed spacings, maybe some crossed out lines, and other oddness that I have left in for the sake of preserving history. I hope you enjoy them and don't find it all too distracting.

Volume 4 coming right up!

Ben Ohmart, editor

November 2017

The Pet Store

	BUSINESS: ORCHESTRA DIRECTLY INTO "SCHOOL DAYS"… FADE FOR…
ANNOUNCER:	And now, Baby Snooks' father has decided on a novel plan. In order that Baby Snooks shouldn't write about the fact that "Daddy and Mummy was fighting all day" he is taking Snooks to a pet shop to buy her a pet so Snooks can write a composition about her experience with her new pet. Here they are—Baby Snooks and her father in front of a pet shop.
FATHER:	Now Snooks, I'm going to buy you a little pet so you'll have something to write about for school. Before we go into the pet shop I want to know what kind of an animal you'd like.
BRICE:	I want an animal that could swim.
FATHER:	All right, then I'll buy you a fish.
BRICE:	But I want it should also climb a tree.
FATHER:	Then you want a squirrel.
BRICE:	Yeah, but I want it should also sing.
FATHER:	Well, in that case you want a canary.
BRICE:	Uh-huh. And I want it to ride on wheels.

FATHER:	Now wait a minute, Snooks—there's no animal that can do all these things.
BRICE:	Yes there is.
FATHER:	What animal can swim, climb a tree, sing and ride on wheels?
BRICE:	Me!
FATHER:	Now stop this nonsense and let's go into the shop and pick out a nice pet.
	BUSINESS: DOOR SLAM
WOMAN:	How do you do, Miss. What can I do for you, Sir?
FATHER:	My little daughter would like to buy a pet.
WOMAN:	Would you like a nice little dog?
BRICE:	Daddy, would I like a nice little dog?
FATHER:	Of course.
BRICE:	No, I wouldn't.
FATHER:	All right, then what do you want?
BRICE:	I want a rabbit that barks.
FATHER:	A rabbit that barks? See here, Snooks, rabbits don't bark.
BRICE:	Yes they do.
FATHER:	Whoever gave you that idea?
BRICE:	It says so in my story book.
FATHER:	What does it say in your story book?
BRICE:	Rabbits eat cabbage and bark.

FATHER:	Oh, that's different—that's the bark of a tree.
BRICE:	Does a tree bark too?
FATHER:	Don't you understand—there are two kinds of bark. The bark of a dog is a sound—and the bark of a tree is a cover.
BRICE:	And what's the bark of a rabbit?
FATHER:	Don't you understand—rabbits eat the bark of a tree.
BRICE:	Could you eat a snore?
FATHER:	What kind of an idiotic question is that? How could I eat a snore?
BRICE:	Then how could a rabbit eat a bark?
FATHER:	Listen, Snooks, do you want me to buy you something or give you a spanking?
BRICE:	Waaaahhhhh!
FATHER:	What are you crying about?
BRICE:	'Cause I know which I'm gonna get!
FATHER:	Well if you're a nice girl you won't get a spanking.
MAN:	Now little girl, would you like a little fish in a bowl?
BRICE:	Daddy, would I like a little fish in a bowl?
FATHER:	No!
BRICE:	Yes I would!
WOMAN:	Now here's a tank full of all kinds of fish. Would you like this pretty catfish?

BRICE: NO!

MAN: Why not?

BRICE: 'Cause you got to put it out every night.

FATHER: Snooks, make up your mind what kind of fish you'd like.

BRICE: Daddy?

FATHER: What?

BRICE: Is there rich fish and poor fish?

FATHER: Of course not.

BRICE: Yes there is.

FATHER: Who told you there are rich fish and poor fish?

BRICE: You did!

FATHER: When did I ever say that?

BRICE: When you called Uncle Robert a poor fish!

FATHER: Snooks, I'm going to spank you!

WOMAN: Don't lose your temper, sir. I know just how to handle the little girl. Now if you want the fish, little girl, this little bowl goes with it and you get all the plants and scenery in it.

BRICE: What's scenery?

WOMAN: Well, scenery is anything that grows in nature.

BRICE: Is that wart on your nose scenery?

WOMAN: Well, I never—I—

FATHER: Don't lose your temper, Miss—I know just how to

	handle the little girl... Snooks, do you want that fish?
BRICE:	To eat it?
FATHER:	No—no—as a pet.
BRICE:	Could I take it to school with me?
FATHER:	Well, you don't expect to carry a bowl full of water to school with you every day and you certainly can't take the fish out of the water.
BRICE:	Why?
FATHER:	Because a fish only breathes under water.
BRICE:	Could I breathe under water?
FATHER:	No—of course not!
BRICE:	Yes I can. I once breathed for a whole hour under water.
FATHER:	Stop that nonsense—you never breathed for a whole hour under water.
BRICE:	I did so!
FATHER:	When was that?
BRICE:	When I was standing under the shower.
FATHER:	That's different—you were getting air through the water.
BRICE:	Well, don't the fish get air through the water?
FATHER:	Yes. But fish are the only animals that can breathe air through water.
BRICE:	Waaahhhh!
FATHER:	Why are you crying?

BRICE:	'Cause I'm a fish and you never told me!
FATHER:	Now you've got to get home and write your composition. You can write about the fish and the bowl and how daddy bought it for you, can't you?
BRICE:	Uh-huh.
FATHER:	That's fine. Now miss—pack up the fish in the bowl.
WOMAN:	Yes sir. Would the little girl like this nice little angora kitten?
BRICE:	Ooooh—I want it!
FATHER:	You can't have it, Snooks.
BRICE:	I want to write a composition about the kitten.
FATHER:	Just stick to the fish. The kitten is too expensive.
BRICE:	Why?
FATHER:	Don't ask any more questions.
BRICE:	Why?
FATHER:	Snooks, I want you to be quiet and don't say another word until you're spoken to.
WOMAN:	Here you are, sir—here's the fish bowl all wrapped up. That'll be $2.
FATHER:	Here's the money.
WOMAN:	Thank you.
FATHER:	Come on, Snooks.
	BUSINESS: DOOR SLAM

BRICE:	Daddy.
FATHER:	Didn't I tell you not to speak until you're spoken to?
BRICE:	Well, ask me if I got the kitten in my pocket and I'll say "yes".
FATHER:	Good heavens! You'll have to return it at once! At any rate, Snooks, now you've had so many things happen to you that you'll be able to write your composition on how you spent the day at home, won't you?
BRICE:	Uh-huh.
FATHER:	How will you start the composition? Now let me hear.
BRICE:	Well—er—er—Daddy and Mummy was fighting all day!
	BUSINESS: APPLAUSE...

A Night Snack
Undated Script

ANNOUNCER: Snooks, by way of a change, has been very naughty, and Daddy, thinking it high time for action has sent her to bed without her supper... But after a little deliberation he decides that he may have been a little too hasty - so to make it up he has prepared a little snack to bring up to her ... We pick Daddy up as he tiptoes quietly into Snooks' room, and prepares to awaken her gently.

DADDY: (WHISPERS) Snooks... Snooks - wake up.

BRICE: Ssshhh.

DADDY: (WHISPERS) I've brought you -

BRICE: Sssshhhhh.

DADDY: (WHISPERS) What's the matter?

BRICE: I'm sleepin'.

DADDY: But I went to all the trouble of making you this nice sandwich – are you sure you don't want it?

BRICE: What's in it?

DADDY: Some roast beef, pimento cheese, sliced tomato, chopped olives, butter and anchovies.

BRICE: I don't want any butter.

DADDY:	All right - I'll scrape the butter off... First I'll lift up the tomatoes, then the olives - oops, there went the tomatoes! ... Oh, well, you don't need them... Now let me see - where are the chopped olives?
BRICE:	On your vest, Daddy.
DADDY:	Huh? Oh, yes - so they are... There - now I've scraped off all the butter.
BRICE:	You better scrape it off your tie, too.
DADDY:	Never mind – here's your sandwich.
BRICE:	Where's the pimento cheese?
DADDY:	It was mixed in with the butter so I had to take them both off… Go on, eat your sandwich.
BRICE:	I don't like rye bread.
DADDY:	That's white bread.
BRICE:	I don't like white bread, either.
DADDY:	Well, what kind of bread do you like?
BRICE:	Toast.
DADDY:	It's too late now – you'll have to eat it the way it is.
BRICE:	Can't I eat it without bread?
DADDY:	Whoever heard of a sandwich without bread? You've gotta have something to keep the food together.
BRICE:	What food?
DADDY:	Well, the roast beef and – and – well, the roast beef!
BRICE:	You're standing on it, Daddy.

DADDY:	Now look what you've done with petty peeves.
BRICE:	I want some pretty peas.
DADDY:	Stop it and eat your sandwich.
BRICE:	There's nothing in it.
DADDY:	Oh… Well, drink this nice big glass of milk.
BRICE:	No – I want a nice big glass of beer.
DADDY:	Forget it, you're too young – beer is for big girls.
BRICE:	Is Uncle Louie a big girl?
DADDY:	Snooks, if you don't promise to behave I'll go downstairs for my belt and spank you good… Now will you promise?... (PAUSE)... Promise?
BRICE:	Will you bring up some beer while you're down there?
DADDY:	Drink your milk!
BRICE:	All right, if you'll drink some beer.
DADDY:	I don't want any beer – I'm full.
BRICE:	You full of beer?
DADDY:	No!... I just had my dinner, and was reading in my study when I suddenly felt sorry for you... Why, I'll never know!
BRICE:	What was you reading?
DADDY:	Freud on Dreams.
BRICE:	I want some fried dreams.
DADDY:	It isn't anything to eat – it's a book on Dream Analysis.

BRICE: Tell me about her.

DADDY: Tell you about who?

BRICE: Analysis in Wonderland. (LAUGHS)

DADDY: Very funny... Now go to sleep.

BRICE: Awight... Goodnight.

DADDY: Goodnight.

BRICE: Daddy.

DADDY: What is it now?

BRICE: Gimme me something to dream about.

DADDY: How in the world can I do that?

BRICE: You got a whole book full of 'em.

DADDY: Those are merely dream interpretations – they only tell you the meanings of the dreams.

BRICE: Can you tell the meanings of dreams?

DADDY: Why - uh – I think so.

BRICE: All right – what am I dreaming of?

DADDY: You can't dream without sleeping!

BRICE: Can you sleep without dreaming?

DADDY: No.

BRICE: I did.

DADDY: What did you dream?

BRICE: I dreamed I took your watch and tried to open my bank with it -

DADDY: Go on.

BRICE: – and I broke your watch in a million pieces.

DADDY: You were asleep when you dreamed that.

BRICE: Was I?

DADDY: Yes... You see, dreams are all part of the subconscious mind. Your dream was merely wish fulfillment – your subconscious mind took care of your conscious desire and carried out your act in your dream.

BRICE: Well?

DADDY: Well what?

BRICE: Ain't you gonna spank me?

DADDY: (LAUGHS) Of course not – the whole thing is just a figment of your imagination.

BRICE: I want some fig mints.

DADDY: I said figment – it means the whole thing is in your mind. You only imagine you broke my watch... Grasp?

BRICE: Grass, Daddy.

DADDY: What?

BRICE: You see that little pile of junk on my bureau?

DADDY: Yes – why?

BRICE: That's your watch.

DADDY: You broke my watch!

BRICE: I did it when I was unconscious.

DADDY:	You incorrigible child - now you're going to get it good... Turn over.
BRICE:	Waaaaaah!
DADDY:	Crying isn't going to help you this time – you broke my watch, and you're going to be spanked for it.
BRICE:	Will you promise not spank me if I didn't break your watch?
DADDY:	You mean that jumbled mass of junk isn't my watch?
BRICE:	Will you promise not to spank me?
DADDY:	Yes, if it isn't my watch.
BRICE:	Well it isn't.
DADDY:	Thank heavens!
BRICE:	It's your fountain pen and glasses.
DADDY:	That settles it - turn over.
BRICE:	But you promised!
DADDY:	I don't care - Oh, all right... Now go to sleep before I change my mind.
BRICE:	Goodnight, Daddy.
DADDY:	Goodnight... You won't disturb me anymore – I'm going to lock your door... (KEY TURNS IN LOCK... DADDY'S FOOTSTEPS GOING DOWNSTAIRS)
DADDY:	Ahhh – back in my study at last... Now, let me see - what page was I on? Oh, here it is...
BRICE:	Hello, Daddy!

DADDY:	Snooks!... How did you get down here – I locked you in your room.
BRICE:	I got out through a secret hole in the window.
DADDY:	There's no hole in the window!
BRICE:	There is now.
DADDY:	Snooks - you didn't -
BRICE:	No, I didn't - the window was open... I just tied my bedsheets together and climbed down them.
DADDY:	You're lying to me.
BRICE:	Only partly.
DADDY:	Which part did you lie about?
BRICE:	The part about climbing down my bedsheets.
DADDY:	Well, how did you get down here?
BRICE:	I dreamed I was a fly and flew through the keyhole.
DADDY:	Uh-huh.
BRICE:	Daddy – why are you taking off your slipper?
DADDY:	I'm dreaming I'm a fly-swatter... Now, will you go back to bed or must I -
BRICE:	I'll go to bed if you'll tell me just one dream.
DADDY:	All right, I'll tell you what I dreamed last night – and then we'll see if we can interpret it.
BRICE:	Goody... Go on, Daddy.

DADDY: Well, I saw nature open her sky picture for me page by page... I saw the lambent flame of dawn leaping across the livid east - the red-stained sulphurous islets floating in the lake of fire in the west - the ragged clouds at midnight, black as raven's wings, blotting out the shuddering moon.... Now, do you know what means?

BRICE: Uh-huh.

DADDY: What?

BRICE: You had a hangover!

DADDY: Oh, go to bed!

BRICE: (LAUGHS)

MUSIC: *CHASER.*

Daddy Invents Water
(January 18, 1940)

MAXWELL HOUSE
GOOD NEWS OF 1940
January 18, 1940

1. "Confucius Say"
2. Arnold-Willson-Gargan "Scatterbrain"   Connie Boswell
3. Commercial
4. Baby Snooks   Fanny Brice And Hanley Stafford
5. "Madam Sherry"   Orch & Chorus
6. Arnold-Rubin-Lane-Gargan
7. Station Break
8. "Love Is Just A Cheat"   Orch & Chorus
9. "Joe And Ethel Turp Go To See "Gone With The Wind"
10. "Things You Are"   Connie Boswell
11. Snooks Spot—Commercial
12. Concert Hall   Orch & Chorus
13. Sign-Off

HULL: Maxwell House Coffee presents...Good News of 1940!

    MUSIC: IN AND FADE

ARNOLD:	This is Edward Arnold, and on behalf of the makers of Maxwell House Coffee I welcome you to another hour of Good News brought to you from Hollywood, starring Fanny Brice, Connie Boswell, Hanley Stafford, Frank Travis, Benny Rubin, and Meredith Willson and his orchestra. Tonight's guests of honor are William Gargan, who will present another of Damon Runyon's Joe Turp stories, and Miss Lola Lane who, as all the world knows, is one of the charming Lane Sisters who have been lending their talents to the Warner Brothers pictures recently. Now our first number is a little novelty entitled "Confucius Say," and unless Meredith Willson wants to make a statement, I don't see why we shouldn't get started.
MEREDITH:	Got a statement, Ed. The way I figure it, the music is more enjoyable if you have a little of the background.
ARNOLD:	Well, that's one way of looking at it. Myself, I prefer just to shut my eyes while you're playing, and dream about a nice cup of Maxwell House Coffee.
MEREDITH:	It wouldn't fit with this song, Ed. Here's my statement, as follows: "The Song 'Confucius Say' is based upon the philosophy of the great Chinese thinker Confucius, who lived from 550 to 478 B.C., new paragraph." Don't know why the girl typed *that* in, too. "Confucius was the father of Confucianism, which was popular during the Han Dynasty, look up Dynasty." Oh Fiddle Faddle, I'll have to replace that secretary.
ARNOLD:	Well, why don't you?
MEREDITH:	I'm afraid Peggy wouldn't like it. That's Mrs. Willson.

ARNOLD: You poor fellow, you mean you can't even fire your secretary without hearing from your wife?

MEREDITH: Well, it ain't so easy when your wife is your secretary. Leave me alone, I'm gonna finish my statement.

ARNOLD: All right. Is there much more?

MEREDITH: No. "The song Confucius Say was not written by Confucius. It was written by Carmen Lombardo and Cliff Friend. It is my earnest hope that these few remarks will make the number more enjoyable to all, applause." Oh, nuts, I better play it!

ARNOLD: Yes, for heaven's sake play it!

"CONFUCIUS SAY"—ORCH AND CHORUS

(APPLAUSE)

ARNOLD: Very good, Meredith!

MEREDITH: That's what I thought, too.

GARGAN: I wonder what Confucius thought.

ARNOLD: Well—Bill Gargan! Hello!

MEREDITH: Hi Bill!

GARGAN: Hello boys! Say, I want to tell you what happened to me last night driving in from Santa Monica. I was reading your autobiography yesterday afternoon, Eddie, and I—

ARNOLD: Thanks, William. "Lorenzo Goes To Hollywood," published by Liveright, three dollars.

GARGAN: Okay—it's pretty good, too! But I was thinking last night that if I had to write my autobiography I wouldn't

	have anything exciting to put in it. You know, I'm just one of those guys nothing ever happens to!
MEREDITH:	Something happen, Bill?
GARGAN:	Wait till I tell you. I was driving in late last night, and I got to that place on Wilshire near that what-do-you-call-it, the Old Soldiers Home, and just as I was gonna turn I saw a—
MEREDITH:	You mean the North end of the home, or the South end?
GARGAN:	Oh, you know, where San Vicente comes into Wilshire.
MEREDITH:	I see.
GARGAN:	The lights had just changed, and I was just starting into Wilshire, when I—
MEREDITH:	That would be the South end of the Old Soldiers Home.
GARGAN:	I guess so. Anyway, just as I was starting, I saw a guy standing in front of me, and he thumbs me for a ride. Well, he looked okay, except he was wearing one of those deer-stalker caps, so I stopped and let him in. But as soon as he got in the car I noticed he—
MEREDITH:	That's the kind of a hat Sherlock Holmes wears, isn't it?
GARGAN:	Yes. (PAUSE)
MEREDITH:	Go ahead, Bill.
GARGAN:	Thanks. I noticed the fellow had—
MEREDITH:	I didn't mean to interrupt.
GARGAN:	(HOLLERS) The guy had two fingers missing!
ARNOLD:	Go ahead, Bill, never mind Willson.

GARGAN.	Okay. We drove about a block, and—
MEREDITH:	I didn't do anything. (PAUSE)
GARGAN:	(SPEEDING UP) We'd gone about a block when we passed under a street light, and I saw a gun in the guy's pocket. Naturally, that made me a little nervous, so—
MEREDITH:	Revolver?
GARGAN:	Pistol. He had his hand on it, too, so of course I—
MEREDITH:	Right hand?
GARGAN:	Left hand. Just then we were coming into that lighted part of Wilshire, so I began looking around for a—
MEREDITH:	Westwood?
GARGAN:	READ IT IN MY AUTOBIOGRAPHY! I can't stand this, Eddie, I'll see you later. (HE DUCKS)
ARNOLD:	Meredith, you're certainly very trying.
MEREDITH:	What did I do? I was just getting interested in the story.
ARNOLD:	Why don't you just stick to music for a while? For instance I know a lot of people would just love to hear Connie Boswell sing "Scatterbrain." And Connie, I happen to be one of 'em.
CONNIE:	Thank you sir. Come on, Meredith, Cheer up!
	"SCATTERBRAIN"—BOSWELL & ORCH
	(APPLAUSE)

ARNOLD:	Say Warren.
HULL:	Yes, Eddie.
ARNOLD:	You know, Warren...every time I see the picture of the old Maxwell House on that familiar blue coffee can...I begin wondering what that famous hotel *was like*...at the height of its glory.
HULL:	Well, Eddie...go back with me fifty years...and I'll take you on an inspection tour. (MUSIC CREEPS IN)
	Together we enter the magnificent lobby paved in blocks of black and white marble...with a fountain in the center...and a gallery running around three sides. At the top of a richly carpeted staircase...we find the main dining room...two stories high...almost two hundred feet long. The room is aglow with the light of many candles and the loveliness of gracious Southern ladies dressed in crinoline, lace and satin. (MUSIC STARTS FADING) To our right are the kitchens, the carving room, the fruit room and the wine room. (MUSIC OUT) But now let's go into a very special room...a room where the coffee is brewed. As we enter, Old Jerry, the man in charge is saying:
MAN:	(NEGRO DIALECT) Ever since we've been gettin' dis here new blend of cawfee from Massa Joel Cheek (CHUCKLE)...we sure do serve a lot of cawfee!
HULL:	Yes...that's the Maxwell House as it was more than fifty years ago. And because it was the home of the finest cuisine in all the South, Joel Cheek named his superb new coffee blend...Maxwell House...after the hotel. Since that time, the fame of Maxwell House Coffee has spread

across the length and breadth of America!

Today, more people are enjoying this wonderfully delicious coffee than ever before in its history! Today you'll find Maxwell House in more stores than any other coffee in America. Why? Because...this famous coffee is actually richer, more delicious, more downright satisfying than ever before!

If you haven't tried Maxwell House lately, you're missing the matchless flavor of a wonderfully improved blend... you're missing true, natural coffee goodness brought to its peak by the uniform Radiant Roast process.

Yes...fifty years of experience have packed a lot of extra pleasure and satisfaction into that familiar blue can!

So try a pound today, won't you? Discover for yourself why today, this famous coffee is now...more than ever... Good to the Last Drop!

MUSIC BRIDGE

ARNOLD: And now, ladies and gentlemen, here is Fanny Brice as Baby Snooks!

(MUSIC...APPLAUSE)

ARNOLD: For many years Daddy, played by Hanley Stafford, has been interested in chemistry. In fact, he has a small laboratory set up in the basement and you can find him there most any evening, tinkering with his test-tubes and whatnot. Tonight Daddy is at his little bench, experimenting. Listen.

(CLINK OF GLASS)

FATHER:	Hmm-mm. Well! There it is! Yes sir—there it is! I'm really proud of myself!
BRICE:	Hello, daddy.
FATHER:	Hello, Snooks. Have a look at this.
BRICE:	I'm looking, daddy.
FATHER:	You know how I did it?
BRICE:	No.
FATHER:	You see that little tank? That contains hydrogen. The other tank contains oxygen—they're both gases. I took twelve hundred and forty parts of the hydrogen and six hundred and twenty parts of oxygen and mixed them in a cylinder. Then I wrapped it in a towel and touched it off with a match—it exploded twenty two times—and there's the result! Look at it!
BRICE:	What is it?
FATHER:	A glass of water!
BRICE:	Are you thirsty?
FATHER:	No! I made it myself. It took me three hours to make that glass of water.
BRICE:	Why didn't you get it from the sink?
FATHER:	Anybody can get water from the sink! The trick is to make it yourself.
BRICE:	Why?
FATHER:	Why? What would this world be today if everybody was satisfied to get water from the sink?

BRICE:	I dunno.
FATHER:	What would we do if it weren't for great chemists and physicists like Paracelsus, Archimedes, Newton, Millikan? What would we be doing?
BRICE:	Getting water from the sink.
FATHER:	No! They were men of science. Newton was the first man to discover the law of gravity.
BRICE:	Is it like gravy?
FATHER:	It's a natural law that has to do with things falling down. If you throw a piece of chewing gum up in the air what happens?
BRICE:	It sticks to the ceiling.
FATHER:	I'm talking about outside—where there's no ceiling.
BRICE:	I want some chewing gum, daddy.
FATHER:	Never mind that—I'm trying to explain gravity! Newton discovered that all things have a tendency of attraction to the center of the earth. Everything must fall down!
BRICE:	Like pants?
FATHER:	Yes—pants, too! And Newton proved that was true.
BRICE:	Didn't he have no suspenders?
FATHER:	Yes—he had suspenders! Look at Millikan.
BRICE:	Where?
FATHER:	He's a physicist. He worked for years and years building a very complicated machine that weighed two tons.
BRICE:	To keep his pants up?

FATHER: No—to split the atom. And he finally achieved his goal. I suppose you know what he got when he split the atom.

BRICE: Eve.

FATHER: He got the Nobel Prize!

BRICE: Why?

FATHER: Because of his wonderful achievement. An atom is the smallest particle of matter known to man. In fact, it's so small you can't see it.

BRICE: How do you know it's there?

FATHER: Oh, I know all right.

BRICE: How?

FATHER: Because I've studied all about it. Even when I went to college—my first three years I took dietetics and medicine.

BRICE: Do you feel better now, daddy?

FATHER: I feel fine. Run along and let me work.

BRICE: What you gonna do, daddy?

FATHER: I'm conducting a little experiment and I don't want you to bother me.

BRICE: I won't do nothing.

FATHER: All right. I'll show you how I make steam without any fire.

BRICE: Can you make an ice-cream soda?

FATHER: I'm a chemist not a soda jerker!

BRICE:	Why?
FATHER:	Do you wish to observe this experiment or not?
BRICE:	Observe.
FATHER:	All right! Now watch closely. I'm going to put some iron filings in this little bottle...Now, I add some sulphur—
BRICE:	And some molasses.
FATHER:	No! I add a little water.
BRICE:	Is it gonna be an ice-cream soda?
FATHER:	I told you I'm going to make steam without fire! Look at the bottle. Watch what happens.
	(HISSING)
BRICE:	It's smoking, daddy.
FATHER:	There! That's steam—and see those little particles exploding and shooting out. Just like a volcano! How's that?
BRICE:	No good.
FATHER:	What do you mean! I've made steam without fire! That's caused by spontaneous combustion.
BRICE:	Sponsors bustaneous?
FATHER:	That's close enough. I just wanted to show you how steam is made.
BRICE:	It's just like the kettle!
FATHER:	That's right. And do you know why steam comes out of the kettle?

BRICE:	Uh-huh.
FATHER:	Why?
BRICE:	So mummy can open your letters.
FATHER:	Oh, she does, eh? Well, what does she think she'll find?
BRICE:	You know.
FATHER:	I don't know anything! And what are you making yourself so wise about?
BRICE:	I dunno.
FATHER:	Well, stop it! (Might as well be living with a couple of policemen!)
BRICE:	Huh?
FATHER:	Nothing! Go away and let me work.
BRICE:	What's in this bottle, daddy?
FATHER:	(A DREAMY NOTE CREEPS IN) It's a new kind of poison. I've been working on it a long time.
BRICE:	What you gonna do with it?
FATHER:	Oh—I'll find a use for it.
BRICE:	(SCARED) What are you looking at me for?
FATHER:	Snooks—I'd like to try something—
BRICE:	(QUICKLY) Oh, no you ain't!
FATHER:	Snooks, don't be silly. It has nothing to do with the poison!
BRICE:	Then put the bottle down.

FATHER:	Oh—I didn't even know I was holding it...This stuff happens to be rat poison.
BRICE:	Make a rat, daddy.
FATHER:	I can't make rats!
BRICE:	Why?
FATHER:	Because no chemist, no matter how great he is, can make a living thing. Living things are born and each one has a special use.
BRICE:	What was I born for?
FATHER:	There are some questions that even science can't answer! But, here—I'll show you something. This beaker contains a number of elements.
BRICE:	Elephants?
FATHER:	Elements! They're really basic salts—potassium, magnesium, carbon, sulphur and stuff like that.
BRICE:	Looks awful, don't it?
FATHER:	Snooks—in that beaker there is a man!
BRICE:	Huh?
FATHER:	Startling, isn't it? There's everything in that beaker that goes to make a man—but of course you can't see him.
BRICE:	Is he the little man who wasn't there?
FATHER:	Don't be facetious. You can see how wonderful chemistry really is. You can take a human being and break him down into ninety-eight cents worth of chemicals.

BRICE:	How do you know?
FATHER:	I just did it. Look at the beaker.
BRICE:	There's a man in there?
FATHER:	A complete one. Broken down of course. I've got him in that jar.
BRICE:	A broken-down man?
FATHER:	That's right.
BRICE:	What did you do with his hat?
FATHER:	Oh, it wasn't a man to begin with! It's all the component parts that go to make the whole person. Man is composed of those chemicals.
BRICE:	Well, make him alive, daddy.
FATHER:	I told you it can't be done! Nobody has the power of creation. I can assure you that a man would be a horrible monstrosity—if a chemist made him.
BRICE:	Did a chemist make Uncle Louie?
FATHER:	You leave Uncle Louie out of this!
BRICE:	I didn't say nothing.
FATHER:	You mind keeps wandering all the time! Can't you pay attention to anything I teach you?
BRICE:	Uh-huh.
FATHER:	All right. Now, what's in that jar?
BRICE:	Uncle Louie!
FATHER:	Well—yes, in effect. But it might be anybody. Now, I'm

	going to show you what you can do by using some of the same chemicals and mixing them with others.
BRICE:	You make Aunt Sophie.
FATHER:	No—here's what I make! What is it?
BRICE:	A firecracker.
FATHER:	Right!
BRICE:	Shoot it off, daddy.
FATHER:	I will in a minute. But I want you to understand this is not the same as an ordinary firecracker. This is perfectly safe and harmless.
BRICE:	Did you make it?
FATHER:	Yes—and I intend to make all the fireworks that you'll shoot off on the Fourth of July.
BRICE:	Why?
FATHER:	Because there won't be any danger of you hurting yourself and besides they're cheaper.
BRICE:	Oh. Well, shoot it off.
FATHER:	All right. You hold it and I'll light it.
BRICE:	No—I'm afraid to hold it.
FATHER:	Don't be afraid. I've worked on this thing for months and I know it's perfectly harmless.
BRICE:	Then you hold it and I'll light it.
FATHER:	Okay. And just to show you how safe it is I'll hold it between my teeth. (THRU HIS TEETH) Go on—light it.

BRICE:	Awight.
	SOUND: (MATCH...SLOW HISS AND THEN A FIZZLE)
BRICE:	Nothing happened.
FATHER:	(THRU TEETH) Didn't I tell you!
	(TERRIFIC BLAST...GLASS CRASH)
BRICE:	Safe, ain't it, daddy?
FATHER:	Ohhh! I don't understand—it worked out all right on paper.
BRICE:	Are you hurt?
FATHER:	No. I was going to have that tooth pulled anyway! Come on—let's get out of here!
BRICE:	(LAUGHS)
	(MUSIC...APPLAUSE)
ARNOLD:	Now, a super-special contribution from Meredith and the Orchestra, and I'm happy to announce I've persuaded him not to say anything about it. It's a tune from one of the fine old musicals of twenty-five years ago, "Madam Sherry." If you go that far back, you'll remember the principal song, "A Birth of Passion." All right, Meredith.
	"MADAM SHERRY"—ORCH AND CHORUS
	(APPLAUSE)
ARNOLD:	Very good, Connie. Now, ladies and gentlemen, we continue with a Good News presentation of—

RUBIN: Excuse me, please, if he's not too much trouble, could I direct you to William Gargan, provided somebody knows where she is.

ARNOLD: I beg your pardon?

RUBIN: Thank you. You are familiar with that little anecdote she's illustrate about the Italian farmer?

ARNOLD: What little anecdote?

RUBIN: It seems farmer near Milano have a barn—and the barn she's two miles long, and a half inch wide.

ARNOLD: A barn two miles long and half an inch wide! What does the father keep in it?

RUBIN: Spaghetti. (SHORT LAUGH) It makes me hysterical!

ARNOLD: Me too. Do you mind if I ask—who are you looking for?

RUBIN: Oh excuse me. I'm looking for William Gargan, she's here?

ARNOLD: I'll call her. Say Bill!

GARGAN: Someone looking for me, Eddie?

ARNOLD: This gentleman here. This is Mr. Gargan, sir.

RUBIN: Signor Gargan, permit me to introduce yourself. My name is Giuseppe Roberto Rallentando Zola.

GARGAN: I'm pleased to meet you.

RUBIN: Thank you. You are familiar with that little anecdote?

GARGAN: Little anecdote?

RUBIN:	Precising. It seems there was a travelling salesman who met a nice old lady—just like your grandmamma. He meet her on that beautiful train, the Super Cheese.
GARGAN:	Super Chief.
RUBIN:	Precising. I would not wish to matriculate with you.
GARGAN:	Of course!
RUBIN:	Well—this travelling salesman meets the old lady, and the old lady has no place to sleep because the train is over-populationed. Do I follow you?
GARGAN:	Precising.
RUBIN:	The travelling salesman has a heart of gold, so he offers his sleeping space to the unfortunate female, while he's spend night in cigar room. In the morning he telegraph his wife—Be home five o'clock am very tired. Last night gave berth to old lady. (SHORT LAUGH) It makes me hysterical.
ARNOLD:	Excuse me, Signor Zola, but why do you keep telling jokes at the drop of a hat?
RUBIN:	Oh! You are familiar with that little anecdote about the hat? It seems—
GARGAN:	Wait a minute! What are you here for, if I'm not too indicative?
RUBIN:	The splendor is all mine. I am just complete transatlantic voyage from Napoli first beginning, I am disembark in Brooklyn, that's the last place I wanna be.
GARGAN:	Now wait a minute, Signor, Brooklyn's fine!

RUBIN: Oh sure! That's so nice a place my eyes ever behold. I just mean it's the last place you gonna be when you finish with boat, is it?

GARGAN: Oh, you mean it's the last stop?

RUBIN: Thank you. It's not my intention for you to make a misconscrew. I am arrive in this country just a fortnight.

GARGAN: A fortnight?

RUBIN: Four weeks.

GARGAN: That's what I thought. Who sent you to see me, Mr. Zola?

RUBIN: It is of no consequence. The main thing—I am here, you are there and opportunity knocks but once in a lifebuoy.

GARGAN: Once in a lifebuoy. Er—you don't mean once in a lighthouse?

RUBIN: Thank you. Oh, you are familiar with that little anecdote?

GARGAN: Know it like a brother.

RUBIN: Well, it seems there was once a man who lived in a lighthouse, on a little, small, medium size island.

GARGAN: It wasn't very big.

RUBIN: Big enough for him. He's work in this lighthouse for thirty years—and every morning at three o'clock—is go off a big cannon—BOOM—all by himself.

GARGAN: Automatically.

RUBIN: Precising—I no like to osculate with you.

GARGAN: The feeling is mutual. Go on with the anecdote.

RUBIN: Thank you. Three o'clock every morning this big cannon go off and the lighthouse keeper is so used to the noise—he not even wake up. One morning—she's come three o'clock—something go wrong with the cannon—and he not explode. The man sat up in bed and said, "What was that?"... (SHORT LAUGH)... It's make me hysterical.

GARGAN: Mr. Zola, I don't wish to be rude, but this is a broadcasting station, and we're giving a radio program. Would you mind telling me just what you want?

RUBIN: Signor Gargan, I'll put it in one word. I am offering you the golden opportunity to invest in the Zola Development Company.

GARGAN: That's a long word. How much do you want?

RUBIN: Ah, Signor, with me money is no subject. I must see my dream come true. Possibility it would surprise you to hear that I come from a long family of inventors.

GARGAN: Nothing can surprise me now.

RUBIN: Thank you. My father, Pianissimo Zola, was a professor of electro-dynamics at a big American university.

GARGAN: Which university?

RUBIN: Sing Sing.

GARGAN: That's a nice college. What was your father's title there?

RUBIN: He had the chair of electricity.

GARGAN: Oh, everybody's dying to get that job. And you want to follow in your father's footsteps?

RUBIN: Oh, I could not hope to be so pernicious. All I ever invent so far is the wireless.

GARGAN: Uhuh. Do you know anything about Marconi?

RUBIN: It's very delicious with cheese. Then I invented television. You know what's television—it's a big machine you push your face in the front in Los Angeles, it's come out in the back in Washington.

GARGAN: That's a quite a gimmick. But I don't want to put any money in television right now.

RUBIN: Oh, I'm not ask you for that. With television you can only see the program. But with my new machine you can almost taste it.

GARGAN: That's very tempting. I wouldn't mind Kate Smith with a side order of onions.

RUBIN: Oh, you like onions?

GARGAN: Go on with the invention!

RUBIN: I don't broadcast the taste, Signor. Not précising. My machine she's called Aromacast. She's based on a new principle—Smellavision.

GARGAN: I think the fellow's on the level.

RUBIN: Oh sure! For instance—just think how beautiful it would be when I broadcast the delicious aroma of Maxwell House Coffee, good to the last drip.

GARGAN: That would really sell the coffee like hot cakes!

RUBIN: I'll broadcast hot cakes too. I'll smell up every home in America.

GARGAN: Listen—if you got a machine that really works, you'll make a fortune!

RUBIN: There's only one draw-backwards. You gotta educate the great American public. People in this country not know how to catch up aroma very good.

GARGAN: What do you mean?

RUBIN: Well for instance—everybody's whos's smell delightful aroma smell like this—one, two, three—(SNIFF) That's wrong.

GARGAN: How do you do it?

RUBIN: Not like one, two, three, (SNIFF)—but like this—(SNIFF) two, three, four. May I have your check, please?

GARGAN: Are you familiar with the anecdote about the—

RUBIN: Please! This is no time for jokes! If you invest in my company I pay you great honor. I push your name up on sign right along with me!

GARGAN: I get top billing?

RUBIN: Precising. Think—what a beautiful name! The Gargan-Zola Company!

GARGAN: The Gargan-Zola Company. Well, it fits for smellavision.

RUBIN: Thank you. If you no have the check, I'll take four million dollars in cash.

GARGAN: That's very nice of you, Mr. Zola, but—

MAN: Oh, there he is. Excuse me, sir.

GARGAN: What's this?

MAN: This fella got away from me three times today already. Come on, Professor!

RUBIN: Oh sure! I come quietly. Goodbye, Mr. Gargan!
(KISSES HIM AND GOES)

GARGAN: You certainly meet a lot of broken bottles on this program!

(MUSIC...APPLAUSE)

ARNOLD: Why you poor sap, I knew the guys in the white coat were coming! That's why I ducked out!

GARGAN: You did?

ARNOLD: Precising!

LOLA: Eddie Arnold, will you tell me one thing?

ARNOLD: Why Lola Lane! (APPLAUSE) Anything your heart desires, Lola!

LOLA: I was sitting here just now, listening to Mr. Zola talk to poor Bill—

GARGAN: Don't rub it in, baby!

LOLA: No, Bill! I believed him too! And when he began talking about the aroma of Maxwell House Coffee, I could almost taste it! Now I know you serve coffee on this program—

ARNOLD: That's right.

LOLA: Well where is it? I'm quite sure Bill could use a cup, too!

(INTO STATION BREAK)

STATION BREAK

ARNOLD:	Well, Lola, the clock has reached the half-way point in our proceedings tonight, and that familiar fragrance in the air tells me it's time for our famous Thursday evening custom...(breaking off abruptly). Say, Meredith! What are you doing over there?
HULL:	(LAUGHING) He's observing our custom already, Eddie!
WILLSON:	(COMING ON MIKE) For weeks now, Eddie, I've been pouring out the music while Warren pours the Maxwell House...and this week, well, (WILLSON CHUCKLE) I thought I'd pour my own!
ARNOLD:	Meredith, man knows no temptation quite like a steaming, freshly made cup of Maxwell House Coffee. You're excused! And now, friends, wherever you are... all over America...pull up your chairs and join us in this moment of relaxation over a cup of the coffee that's Good to the Last Drop! Meredith, may I call on you now for the music that goes with it?
WILLSON:	Er, pray do, Eddie! Pray do! MUSIC FULL UP AND FADE FOR
HULL:	We pause briefly for station identification. MUSIC FULL AND FADE...
ARNOLD:	This is Edward Arnold again, and we open the second half of our Maxwell House Good News program with another of Meredith Willson's New Year specials, a brilliant arrangement of the popular song "Love Is Just A Cheat."

"LOVE IS JUST A CHEAT"—ORCHESTRA

(APPLAUSE)

ARNOLD: Recently Metro-Goldwyn-Mayer released one of Damon Runyon's best known stories "Joe and Ethel Turp call on the President" currently showing at your favorite theater with Ann Sothern, William Gargan and Walter Brennan...Two weeks ago we had the pleasure of presenting Bill Gargan and Good News in the role of Joe Turp...So many people who heard the broadcast and saw the picture have requested more of Joe and Ethel Turp that we present another of Damon Runyon's famous Joe Turp letters tonight with William Gargan as Joe, and lovely Lola Lane as Ethel.

"Joe and Ethel Turp go to see 'Gone With the Wind'" by Damon Runyon adapted for radio by Robert Reily Crutcher.

(**Section not written by Philip Rapp has been omitted**)

(MUSIC UP)

(APPLAUSE)

ARNOLD: A grand story, and a marvelous performance!

LOLA AND GARGAN: Thank you, Eddie.

ARNOLD: Lola, you really deserve a medal!

LOLA: Eddie, you can make me happy very easily without having any bronzes struck off!

ARNOLD: Just name it, and it's yours!

LOLA:	Please—please—if Connie Boswell could sing "All the Things You Are"! I'm crazy about Connie, and I'm crazy about the song!
ARNOLD:	My dear, no sooner said than done! Connie—can we have "All The Things you Are"—for Lola Lane?
CONNIE:	Soitenly, Eddie. For you I'd be happy to be berled in erl.
	"ALL THE THINGS YOU ARE"—BOSWELL & ORCHESTRA
	(APPLAUSE)
BRICE:	Daddy?
FATHER:	What is it, Snooks?
BRICE:	Don't Connie Boswell sing wonderful?
FATHER:	You mean wonderfully.
BRICE:	Why?
FATHER:	Because that's better grammar. She sings wonderfully, I sing wonderfully, they sing wonderfully. Wouldn't that be more correct?
BRICE:	No.
FATHER:	Why not?
BRICE:	Cause you don't sing so wonderful.
FATHER:	Well I don't propose to stand here and discuss my bel canto with you.
BRICE:	I didn't say nothing about that.
FATHER:	Oh, we'll talk about it some other time.

MEREDITH:	Excuse me, Daddy.
FATHER:	Oh, hello, Meredith.
BRICE:	Can I lead the band, Mr. Willson?
FATHER:	Stop it, Snooks! If you want to lead the band you've got to know all about music.
BRICE:	Then why is he doing it?
MEREDITH:	Hmph! By the way, Daddy, I've been meaning to talk to you about Snooks's grammar.
FATHER:	Oh, you have?
BRICE:	Oh, you have?
MEREDITH:	Oh—pardon, Snooks. Daddy, I think you should do a little more about teaching your child to say the correct thing.
FATHER:	You think so, huh?
MEREDITH:	Definitely. Why only yesterday I heard her say to a group of children, "My daddy don't never take me nowhere."
FATHER:	Did you say that, Snooks?
BRICE:	Uhuh.
MEREDITH:	There, isn't that awful? Your child goes around saying to people "My daddy don't never take me nowhere."
FATHER:	I'll say it's awful! I take that kid every place I go!
MEREDITH:	Why you're just as bad as she is!
BRICE:	Sock him, daddy!
MEREDITH:	I'll bet you can't even analyze a sentence!

FATHER: When I want grammar lessons I won't come to you! Snooks can analyze any sentence you can!

BRICE: Me too!

MEREDITH: Oh! All right, young lady! I'll give you the simplest possible example. You know what the subjunctive is?

BRICE: Uhuh.

MEREDITH: Okay. "Mary milks the cow." What mood?

BRICE: Huh?

FATHER: Milks the cow. What mood?

BRICE: The cow mooed.

MEREDITH: No, that's not right at all. You have to analyze the sentence. For instance, what does "the cow" stand for?

BRICE: Mary.

FATHER: The cow stands for Mary! Why do you say that?

BRICE: How else could she milk it?

MEREDITH: Hmph! No use wasting my time trying to learn you people grammar!

(WALKS AWAY)

COMMERCIAL

ARNOLD: And now, here's Warren Hull...whose helpful words need no introduction.

HULL: Thanks, Eddie. Friends...let's make believe you're jotting down a list of things you want from the grocer's tomorrow.

WOMAN: (TO HERSELF, SLOWLY, TRYING TO REMEMBER) Now let's see...I need butter...eggs...sugar...coffee.

HULL: (IN FAST) Now that item of coffee, madam. Instead of just writing down coffee, I wish you'd write down Maxwell House Coffee—Drip Grind...or, Maxwell House Coffee—Regular Grind.

WOMAN: Why is that important, Mr. Hull?

HULL: Because...today...with all the different ways of making coffee...it's just as important to get the right *grind* of coffee, as it is the right kind!

WOMAN: I wish you'd explain...

HULL: Well...when you make coffee correctly by the drip method, the water passes through the coffee *just once*! Now that means the coffee you use must be ground just fine enough, so that all the flavor can be extracted in that one contact with the water. And that's just why Maxwell House comes in a special Drip Grind...a grind you can always trust to give you clear, full-bodied flavorful coffee in any type of drip or glass coffee maker.

On the other hand, if you make coffee in a percolator or coffee pot, you know the water comes in contact with your coffee not once, but many times. This means you need the Regular Grind Maxwell House...to stand up in the longer brewing, and give you the rich, satisfying coffee you should expect every day.

Drip or Regular, just ask for the Maxwell House grind that's right for your way of making coffee. We'd like you to discover the extra flavor and economy of *perfect coffee...perfectly ground*!

"THOUGHTS WHILE STROLLING"—FADES FOR...

ARNOLD: In the Concert Hall tonight Meredith Willson presents a song that received its first hearing one hundred years ago...In 1840 Robert Schumann's great song of the Napoleonic Wars, "Two Grenadiers" was acclaimed by music lovers...Through all the intervening years it has been played and sung throughout the Western World, and today it is as popular as ever.

And so we honor it tonight..."The Grenadiers" featuring the voice of Frank Travis.

"TWO GRENADIERS"—TRAVIS, ORCHESTRA AND CHORUS

(APPLAUSE)

ARNOLD: And so, once again Meredith Willson has presented a beloved song whose melody has stood the test of time...And next week, ladies and gentlemen, we have a great show for you. It's Movie Night on Good News... Darryl F. Zanuck joins with Good News in presenting Alice Faye, Richard Greene, Brenda Joyce and an all-star cast in a scene from 20th Century-Fox's new production, "Little Old New York". And to celebrate the occasion, Good News has added George Huston and Jan Duggan, the bowery nightingale, in addition to our regular cast—Fanny Brice as Baby Snooks, with Hanley Stafford as Daddy, Connie Boswell, Meredith Willson and his music, and of course, I'll be tagging along too... So until next Thursday—this is Edward Arnold saying goodnight.

(ALWAYS AND ALWAYS)

HULL: This is Warren Hull, reminding you that leading grocers are now featuring Maxwell House Coffee at new, low prices...prices the most modest budget can afford! Now more than ever is the time to...make friends with Maxwell House!

And now...good night and good luck from the makers of Maxwell House...the coffee that's now...more than ever... Good to the Last Drop.

ANNOUNCER: THIS IS THE NATIONAL BROADCASTING COMPANY.

Baseball
(June 15, 1939)

MAXWELL HOUSE (REVISED) 6-15-39

YOUNG: And now, ladies and gentlemen, here is Fanny Brice as Baby Snooks!

MUSIC: (APPLAUSE)

YOUNG: With Father's Day so close at hand you might think that poor Daddy, played by Hanley Stafford, would be shown a little mercy by his offspring. But Daddy's in worse trouble than ever. Snooks got sick from stuffing herself at a party and Daddy's had to nurse her and put her to bed. On top of that, he's got a date with an out-of-town buyer to see a night baseball game. Here they are!

BRICE: (HOLLERS) Daddy!

FATHER: What's wrong, Snooks?

BRICE: Something's biting me, Daddy.

FATHER: Oh nonsense - it's your imagination. Now go to sleep.

BRICE: I ain't sleepy. Put the light on.

FATHER: Oh, all right. (CLICK) Now, what's biting you?

BRICE: I think it's a turtle.

FATHER:	A turtle? Oh how would a turtle get in your bed?
BRICE:	I brought it home from the party. Here it is.
FATHER:	Why, Snooks! Give me that thing at once! The idea of taking a turtle to bed with you!
BRICE:	Ain't it pretty, Daddy?
FATHER:	Yes it's very pretty - I'm going to put it in some water.
BRICE:	I wanna sleep with it.
FATHER:	(LAUGHS) Oh you can't sleep with a turtle, Snooks, although I know a lady who sleeps with cats.
BRICE:	Who sleeps with cats, Daddy?
FATHER:	Mr. Katz! (LAUGHS LIKE HELL)
BRICE:	(LAUGHS)
FATHER:	(LAUGHS) You get it?
BRICE:	No.
FATHER:	Mrs. Katz - she sleeps with Katz. That's her husband.
BRICE:	Have they got any kittens?
FATHER:	Oh, forget it. Now get back under the covers and I'll put out the lights. Why Snooks, what is this apple doing on the night-table?
BRICE:	It ain't doing nothin', daddy.
FATHER:	I know it isn't. But I told you to take it before you went to sleep.
BRICE:	Why?

FATHER:	Because the doctor wanted to see if you could keep it on your stomach overnight.
BRICE:	I tried. But it kept rolling off.
FATHER:	You were supposed to eat it! Well I guess it's too late now. So go on to sleep.
BRICE:	Where you going, Daddy?
FATHER:	I have an appointment with a buyer.
BRICE:	Buy me something, Daddy.
FATHER:	All right, I'll buy you something. Goodnight - I'm in a hurry.
BRICE:	Will you buy me a bicycle?
FATHER:	No, you can't have a bicycle. You're still too little.
BRICE:	Why?
FATHER:	Now listen, Snooks - when you were five I bought you a tricycle. When you get a little older I'll buy you a bicycle.
BRICE:	When I get real old can have an icicle!
FATHER:	Yes - You can have an icicle!
BRICE:	I want it now!
FATHER:	Oh you can't have an icicle now! Go to sleep - I'm late already!
BRICE:	Where you goin', Daddy?
FATHER:	I'm going to see a night baseball game.
BRICE:	Who with?

FATHER:	I told you - with a buyer! Goodbye!
BRICE:	Goodbye........Daddy!
FATHER:	What is it?
BRICE:	What does he buy?
FATHER:	He buys stuff from my firm. We sell paints and dyes - and this buyer is going to buy some of our dyes.
BRICE:	Why?
FATHER:	Because he needs it in his business!
BRICE:	What's his business, Daddy?
FATHER:	Dying!
BRICE:	Huh?
FATHER:	He's a dyer. He makes his living by dying.
BRICE:	He makes livin' by dyin'?
FATHER:	Yes. He's been dying for thirty years.
BRICE:	Ain't he dead yet?
FATHER:	No. He's not dead. That's just his way of earning a living!
BRICE:	By dyin'?
FATHER:	Yes!
BRICE:	Why don't he get a better job?
FATHER:	Because he likes the job he's got now! Besides, he's a man of fifty and he can't start in a new business.
BRICE:	Can't he?
FATHER:	Why no! If he wants to live he's got to dye!
BRICE:	Do you feel all right, Daddy?

FATHER:	How do you always mange to get me so confused? I can make acceptable explanations to anybody in the world except you!
BRICE:	And Mummy.
FATHER:	Yes - and Mummy. I got myself a fine pair of females!
BRICE:	(LAUGHS) You like us, don't you, Daddy?
FATHER:	Oh of course I like you. But now, I've got to run along to that game – Goodnight, Snooks.
BRICE:	Goodnight, Daddy...........Daddy?
FATHER:	Oh, what is it?
BRICE:	Take me with you.
FATHER:	I knew it was coming! Now Snooks - under no circumstances will I even consider taking you with me tonight!
BRICE:	Waaaahhhhhh!
FATHER:	Oh what are you yelling about?
BRICE:	My tummy hurts.
FATHER:	Well what's the matter with it?
BRICE:	It hurts when I squeeze it.
FATHER:	Well, don't squeeze it.
BRICE:	Then how can I tell if it hurts?
FATHER:	Oh here - drink a little of this warm milk. It'll make you feel better.
BRICE:	What kind of milk is it, Daddy?
FATHER:	Oh what do you mean what kind? It's cow's milk.

BRICE: How does milk get in the cow, Daddy?

FATHER: I don't know. Drink it - I've gotta leave.

BRICE: Does the cow have to drink milk, Daddy?

FATHER: No!

BRICE: Then where does she get it from?

FATHER: From eating grass. A cow eats grass and gives milk.

BRICE: Oh! If the cow ate milk would she give grass?

FATHER: No!

BRICE: Why?

FATHER: Because it - it's much more complicated than that. The grass turns into milk inside the cow's body and it's gathered in hundreds of little ducts.

BRICE: Where are the ducks, Daddy?

FATHER: Inside the cow!

BRICE: Can she hear them when they quack, quack, quack, quack?

FATHER: Oh, I didn't say ducks! I said ducts!

BRICE: Ducts, what's them?

FATHER: They're - they're glands. Let me get out of here!

BRICE: Well, how does the cow get the milk?

FATHER: I told you! Thru the glands - the same way you get your tears when I spank you!

BRICE: Oh.

FATHER:	Now do you understand how you get milk from a cow?
BRICE:	Uh-huh - you gotta spank it!
FATHER:	That's right - give me that glass. Goodnight - I've gotta get to that ball game.
BRICE:	I wanna go with you.
FATHER:	Now Snooks! You get back in bed!
BRICE:	I don't wanna!
FATHER:	If you take one more step I'll spank you!
BRICE:	Go ahead, Daddy - I wanna give some milk!
FATHER:	Ohhh - what am I gonna do with you!
BRICE:	Take me to the ball game.
FATHER:	No!
BRICE:	WaaaaaaaHHHHHHH!
FATHER:	Well you can holler your head off! *I will not take you with me tonight!*
BRICE:	Waaaaaaahhhhhhhh!
	(MUSIC.....APPLAUSE)
YOUNG:	Stand by, ladies and gentlemen - Snooks and Daddy will appear later in the program - and I'm laying eight to five right now they both wind up at the ball game! In the meantime Warren Hull has a word for you....
	(REVISED)

PART TWO

YOUNG: Here she is again, ladies and gentlemen, Fanny Brice as Baby Snooks!

(MUSIC....APPLAUSE)

YOUNG: Just as I predicted, Snooks has wangled Daddy into taking her to the ball game with him. The fourth inning has just started as they enter the ball park. Here they are.

FATHER: Don't drag, Snooks - hang on to my hand. You've given me enough trouble tonight - on account of you I didn't get here till the fourth inning!

BRICE: How do you know, Daddy?

FATHER: Oh it's right up there on the scoreboard. End of the fourth inning and the score is nothing to nothing!

BRICE: Then we didn't miss nothin'

FATHER: Ahh - what do you know! Where the dickens are those ushers?

BRICE: What's those girls in the middle of the field, Daddy?

FATHER: They're not girls - they're men.

BRICE: Then why are they wearing bloomers?

FATHER: Nobody's wearing bloomers!

BRICE: Mummy wears -

FATHER: I don't care about that! Those men are wearing *knockers*!

BRICE: Why?

FATHER:	Because that's part of the baseball player's uniform. Now just follow me, Snooks - I think our seats are right about here.

(CROWD ROARS)

BRICE:	Why is that man runnin', Daddy?
FATHER:	Because he hit the ball.
BRICE:	Does he have to chase it, too?
FATHER:	No he doesn't have to chase it. Oh these are our seats all right but I don't see Mr. Foop.
BRICE:	Who's he?
FATHER:	He's the buyer. I wonder where he is. Oh he left his hat on this seat. Maybe he went to make a phone call.
BRICE:	Maybe he went -
FATHER:	Never mind. He'll be back soon - And I want you to behave and watch the game.
BRICE:	I'll be good, Daddy.
Father:	And don't ask any questions. Just sit here and enjoy yourself.
BRICE:	Awight, Daddy......Daddy?
FATHER:	What is it?
BRICE:	Who's that man in the blue suit?
FATHER:	He's the umpire.
BRICE:	Why is he wearing that wire thing on his face?

FATHER:	To keep from biting the ball players. Now watch the game. The man behind the plate is called the batter.
BRICE:	Why?
FATHER:	Because he holds the bat. The man who's throwing the ball is the pitcher. Now watch him pitch - wham! Strike three!
	(CROWD ROARS)
BRICE:	What happened, Daddy?
FATHER:	The pitcher just fanned the batter.
BRICE:	Was he hot?
FATHER:	No - he struck him out! Just sit still and watch the game. Oh I wonder where Mr. Foop is.
BRICE:	Sit still and watch the game, Daddy.
FATHER:	Huh? Oh. Oh, oh, yes, say – yes, say this pitcher's pretty good. What a wind-up! Wham - right down the middle! What a pitcher!
	(CROWD ROARS)
BRICE:	He's good, ain't he, Daddy? He hit the man's bat with the first shot.
FATHER:	(HOLLERS) Run - Hurry, hurry! Safe!....Ohh - that robber! He called him out!
BRICE:	Who did?
FATHER:	That umpire on first base! The guy was safe by a mile! (Yells) Get a pair of glasses, you big cluck!
BRICE:	Sock him, Daddy!

FATHER:	Ahhh - that was robbery!....Where the dickens is Foop?
BRICE:	I wanna play baseball, Daddy.
FATHER:	You can play tomorrow.
BRICE:	I wanna play here!
FATHER:	Now, stop that nonsense, Snooks. If you get hit with that ball you'll really feel something.
BRICE:	Why?
FATHER:	Because it's made of horsehide.
BRICE:	What did you say, Daddy?
FATHER:	Hide. Hide.
BRICE:	Why should hide?
FATHER:	Hide - the horse's outside!
BRICE:	Bring him in, Daddy - I ain't afraid.
FATHER:	What are you talking about?
BRICE:	(WHINING) I wanna ride on the horsie.
FATHER:	You came to watch a ball game - not ride on horsies! Now stop squirming in your seat and when Mr. Foop gets back I'll talk to him for a few minutes and then we'll go home.
BRICE:	I wanna go home now.
FATHER:	Well you can't go home now. Oh here comes Mr. Foop. And now just remember, Snooks - No cracks.
FOOP:	Oh, hello, Higgins. I just got thru calling your house.

FATHER:	Oh, I'm sorry I was late, Mr. Foop. Er - this is my daughter.
FOOP:	Well! Cute little tyke, isn't she?
FATHER:	Oh, sure.
BRICE:	Where's his hair, daddy?
FATHER:	(THRU CLENCED TEETH) Shut up! Oh - Mr. Foop – Uh, how about coming to my house for dinner tomorrow night?
FOOP:	Well swell. Have you consulted your wife about it?
FATHER:	Oh she knows I'm going to bring you.
BRICE:	Yeah - They had a big fight about it this morning.
FOOP:	What?
FATHER:	Oh! Oh! Pay no attention to the child, Mr. Foop - she's just joking. Wonderful sense of humor. (LAUGHS)
FOOP:	(LAUGHS)
BRICE:	(SAME LAUGH)
FATHER:	Er, pretty good game isn't it?
BRICE:	What happened to your hair, Mr. Poop?
FATHER:	Ohhh! And Mussolini pays a bonus for them!
FOOP:	If you must know, young lady, my hair all fell out. I'm bald!
BRICE:	Does it hurt?
FOOP:	No it doesn't hurt!

BRICE:	Why?
FATHER:	Snooks!
FOOP:	Higgins, did you have to bring this child to the game with you?
FATHER:	Well - er - you see, her mother wasn't home and I didn't want to leave her alone. But she'll be a good girl - (WHEEDLING) Won't you, Snooks?
BRICE:	No, I won't! I wanna be bald!
FOOP:	Now listen - here's a quarter - now don't mention my bald head again, you understand?
BRICE:	Awight.
FATHER:	Oh, don't you dare take that money, Snooks! You don't have to bribe her to be good, Mr. Foop - She can be good for nothing!
FOOP:	Well, she hasn't got far to go!
BRICE:	Waaaahh!
FATHER:	Oh stop your yelling!
BRICE:	Then give me my quarter! I want my bald-headed money!
FOOP:	Oh I'm gonna get out of here! Where's my hat?
FATHER:	Now just a minute, Mr. Foop - please -
FOOP:	My hat! Young lady, do you know what you're sitting on?
BRICE:	(LAUGHS) Shall I tell him, Daddy?
FATHER:	Get off Mr. Foop's hat! Oh I'm terribly sorry about this Mr. -

FOOP:	I know, I know - It's not your fault! Call me tomorrow when you haven't got this little angel with you! Goodnight!
BRICE:	Goodnight, Baldy!
FOOP:	Ohhh!
FATHER:	Well! Are you satisfied now? You're probably wrecked a sale for me! I knew I shouldn't have brought you.
BRICE:	(WHINES) I wanna go home!
FATHER:	You're going to sit here and watch this game!
BRICE:	Then I'll bawl all night!
FATHER:	Go ahead and bawl - and I'll give you the baseball treatment.
BRICE:	What's that?
FATHER:	Four bawls and you'll get your base warmed! Like this! (SLAP)
BRICE:	Waaaahhhh!
	(MUSIC....APPLAUSE)

New Baby
(June 22, 1939)

                    MAXWELL HOUSE COFFE TIME
                        June 22, 1939 (REVISED)

YOUNG: And now ladies and gentlemen, here is Fanny Brice as Baby Snooks!

(MUSIC... APPLAUSE)

YOUNG: Well, there's really been a great event in the Snooks household. Daddy played by Hanley Stafford is swelling with pride because there is a new addition to the family - a bouncing baby boy. But there always has to be something to mar Daddy's happiness. And this time Snooks has disappeared. She hasn't been seen since nine o'clock this morning and Daddy is on the phone, frantic. Listen.

FATHER: Yes, sergeant - she was wearing a little cotton dress and white shoes and she had a blue ribbon in her -

(DOOR SLAM)

Oh wait a minute - I think she's here! Yes! Never mind - Goodbye!... Oh! Snooks!

BRICE: (TIRED) Hello Daddy.

FATHER: Why Snooks, dear. Where have you been all day?

BRICE: I runned away.

FATHER: Oh we've been terribly worried. Are you all right - have you eaten?

BRICE: Uh-huh. Ain't you gonna spank me?

FATHER: Spank you? Have you heard what's happened here? I came home and found you have a new baby brother!

BRICE: I know. That's why I runned away.

FATHER: Well - well what for?

BRICE: 'Cause I get the blame for everything.

FATHER: (LAUGHS) But we're all so happy! You should be thrilled - he's a wonderful baby brother!

BRICE: Does Mummy know about him?

FATHER: Why of course she knows! Mummy brought him home.

BRICE: Where did she get him?

FATHER: Er - the stork brought him. Well, don't you want to see the baby?

BRICE: No - I wanna see the stork.

FATHER: Now stop this silly nonsense. Come up and see your new brother.

BRICE: I seen him, Daddy. Before I runned away.

FATHER: Oh, you did? Well, what do you think of him?

BRICE: He's no good.

FATHER: Now why do you say that?

BRICE:	He ain't got no hair - and he ain't got no teeth.
FATHER:	Why of course not. That's because he's a new baby.
BRICE:	I think they fooled you, Daddy - he looks like a retread.
FATHER:	(LAUGHS) Why, Snooks - I think you're jealous!
BRICE:	No, I ain't. (PAUSE) Are you gonna keep him?
FATHER:	I think so.
BRICE:	Oh...(DISAPPOINTED).... Well I suppose you know what you're doin'.
FATHER:	Why, you'll get to love him soon. And what a boy! He's got Mummy's complexion - and he's got my nose and chin - and he's got grandpa's eyes.
BRICE:	Ain't he got nothin' of his own?
FATHER:	Ahh - he's a little angel. I've never been so proud in my whole life. (LAUGHS HAPPILY)
BRICE:	What's his name, Daddy?
FATHER:	Well, we haven't decided yet. Mother and I thought we'd name him after Uncle Louie....Have you got any suggestions?
BRICE:	Uh-huh.
FATHER:	Oh, good. What would you call him?
BRICE:	Stinky.
FATHER:	Now, Snooks - is that a nice name for your little brother?
BRICE:	I like it.
FATHER:	I simply can't understand your attitude, Snooks. I

	thought you'd be overcome with joy - after all, I know you've been praying for a baby sister for ever so long.
BRICE:	Is he a boy, Daddy?
FATHER:	Why certainly he's a boy.
BRICE:	How do you know?
FATHER:	Snooks, I think you're a little tired - maybe you'd better go to bed now and in the morning you'll feel better.
BRICE:	Awight........Daddy?
FATHER:	What is it?
BRICE:	Did your Daddy know you was boy?
FATHER:	Why, yes.
BRICE:	Why?
FATHER:	Because he did!
BRICE:	How did he know you wasn't a girl?
FATHER:	Because little boys wear pants and little girls wear dresses.
BRICE:	Was you born with clothes on?
FATHER:	Oh, come on to bed........Now get into you pajamas quickly - I have a lot of things to do. Goodnight.
BRICE:	Goodnight....Daddy?
FATHER:	Yes?
BRICE:	If the baby hollers will you spank it?
FATHER:	Well I should say not!

BRICE:	Why?
FATHER:	Well, because you don't spank infants. Besides the baby will only cry when he's hungry.
BRICE:	No, he won't.
FATHER:	Well, what do you mean?
BRICE:	He hollers when you stick a pin in him.
FATHER:	How do you know?
BRICE:	I tried it.
FATHER:	Snooks!
BRICE:	(QUICKLY) I'm only fooling, Daddy. (LAUGHS)
FATHER:	Well, don't you fool like that - you must be awfully careful with the child. And listen, Snooks - I don't want you to think that I enjoy spanking you, either.
BRICE:	Don't you, Daddy?
FATHER:	Why certainly not. As a matter of fact, it hurts me more than it hurts you.
BRICE:	But not in the same place.
FATHER:	Well, never mind that - just be a nice little girl and we'll get along fine. Goodnight.
BRICE:	Goodnight, Daddy........Daddy?
FATHER:	Now what is it?
BRICE:	Does Indians have babies?
FATHER:	Why yes. Indians have babies.
BRICE:	Why?

FATHER: Well how do I know? Go to sleep.

BRICE: I got a picture of an Indian baby, Daddy.

FATHER: Well that's fine.

BRICE: His mama carries him in a golf bag.

FATHER: Yes - that's an old Indian custom. The Indian Daddy is called a brave and the mummy is called a squaw.

BRICE: Squaw!

FATHER: Yes, and you know what Indian babies are called?

BRICE: Squawkers?

FATHER: No - it's a papoose. Tomorrow I'll tell you all about it.

BRICE: No, tell me now.

FATHER: No - I want you to go to sleep this instant!

BRICE: Daddy!

FATHER: Oh, Snooks - what do you want?

BRICE: If a baby is born in America is it an American?

FATHER: Why yes.

BRICE: And if it's born in France is it French?

FATHER: Yes of course.

BRICE: And if it's born in the middle of the ocean what is it?

FATHER: If a baby is born in the middle of the ocean it would be the same nationality as the father or mother.

BRICE: Suppose there was nobody there except the baby's uncle?

FATHER:	Then it would be a miracle - goodnight.
BRICE:	Goodnight......Daddy?
FATHER:	I'm not going to stay here another second!
BRICE:	Waaahhh!
FATHER:	Oh stop that yelling! Do you want to wake up the baby?
BRICE:	Then tell me a story.
FATHER:	No stories tonight - I'm completely worn out! We don't have a baby in this house every day, you know!
BRICE:	Why?
FATHER:	Oh, go to sleep!
BRICE:	I wanna ask you sumpin', Daddy.
FATHER:	Well - what do you want to ask me?
BRICE:	(STALLING) Um - er -- um ----
FATHER:	Well, go on ahead and ask me!
BRICE:	I didn't think of it yet.
FATHER:	Oh sure. All you want to do is keep me here all night so you won't have to go to sleep. Now, I'll allow you to ask me one more question - but that's all.
BRICE:	Awight.
FATHER:	Well go ahead and make it fast.
BRICE:	Who was the first baby?
FATHER:	Oh you know as well as I do. It was Adam - although when he was created he was a full grown man.

BRICE: Was he?

FATHER: Oh now, Snooks - you learned the whole story in Sunday school. About the Garden of Eden - and the serpent - and don't you remember Adam was punished for eating the forbidden fruit?

BRICE: Uh-huh.

FATHER: What was his punishment?

BRICE: He got a wife.

FATHER: No - it was nothing of the kind! And I've done enough talking here - goodnight.

BRICE: Goodnight, Daddy.

FATHER: Oh, have you said your prayers?

BRICE: No.

FATHER: Well say them and I'll turn the light out.

BRICE: Awight. Bless Mummy and bless Daddy and bless Uncle Louie and bless Soph - Aunt Sophie and bless the dog - Amen.

FATHER: Snooks - are you going to leave out your new baby brother?

BRICE: Uh-huh. I don't like him.

FATHER: Oh, Snooks - I'm terribly surprised and hurt. You do love him, don't you?

BRICE: No.

FATHER: But why not?

BRICE:	'Cause nobody likes me anymore.
FATHER:	Oh don't be foolish, child - we all love you as much as ever.
BRICE:	As much as the baby?
FATHER:	Why of course. Now go on - say it.
BRICE:	And bless baby brother.... and make everybody like me best. Amen. Sing me to sleep, Daddy.
FATHER	Oh sure. (SINGS) Rockabye Baby – On The Tree Top -

(MUSIC IN SLOWLY)

(APPLAUSE)

Snooks at the Museum
(for TV, April 17, 1949)

                    BABY SNOOKS

                    (For Telecasting KNBH – April 17, 1949)

                    After titles, credits, etc.

                    FADE IN

                    CLOSE SHOT OF A DIARY

                    The diary, plainly labeled "Daddy's Diary – Personal – Strictly Private" is opened to a blank page, a hand begins to write, and FATHER'S VOICE is heard over the scene.

FATHER'S VOICE:

                    (as he writes) Saturday, April 16 . . . That was yesterday, and I had Snooks on my hands for the entire day . . . Sometimes I wish I had never been born . . . Or Snooks either, for that matter...

                    CLOSE SHOT – FATHER

                    As he writes. He looks haggard, and writes grimly.

FATHER:

                    (slowly, deliberately) My dear wife decided to give a bridge party and chased me out of the house with Snooks...

DISSOLVE TO EXT. STREET

SNOOKS and FATHER stand in front of an ice-cream parlor and candy shop. The window display features a huge chocolate rabbit and an ever larger Easter egg. FATHER is trying to pull SNOOKS away. Two or three pedestrians pass by and look at them curiously.

FATHER: (between his teeth) I said you can't have that rabbit! Now come on.

BRICE: I don't wanna.

FATHER: Please, Snooks—

BRICE: No. I want that rabbit.

FATHER: No!

BRICE: I want that rabbit!

FATHER: (pleading) Listen, Snooks — I took you to the park and you had three tons of ice-cream. I took you to the zoo and you ate all the peanuts and crackerjacks in sight. I took you for a long street-car ride and you ate seventeen packages of bubble gun! What more do you want?

BRICE: I want that rabbit!

FATHER: Well, you can't have it! You'll get sick!

BRICE: (with a dizzy expression) I _am_ sick.

FATHER: (taking her by the hand) Good. I'll take you to the hospital.

BRICE: (pulling away again) No. You didn't buy me nothing for Easter.

FATHER: Easter isn't until tomorrow.

BRICE: Why?

FATHER: (giving up) All right. Let's go in the store. I'll buy you something for Easter.

INT. OF STORE. (CANDY COUNTER)

As they enter.

BRICE: Oooh, lookit all the stuff!

FATHER: Never mind that. I'll buy you one small Easter egg.

BRICE: I want some jelly beans and some lollipops and fudge and some peppermint sticks and some —

FATHER: You want the whole store but you can't have it!

BRICE: Why?

FATHER: Don't torment me. You can have one thing – now what do you want?

BRICE: (pointing off) I want that thing over there.

FATHER: That's a soda jerk!

BRICE: I like him.

FATHER: Getting more like your mother every day!

A salesman walks into scene, behind counter.

SALESMAN: (pleasantly) Yes sir?

FATHER: I want the smallest Easter egg you've got.

BRICE: And I want that chocolate rabbit in the window.

FATHER: You can't have that! That thing weighs twenty-five pounds. You can't even carry it!

BRICE:	I'll eat it here.
FATHER:	Oh, don't be silly, Snooks. It's only for display. That rabbit's not for sale, is it, mister?
SALESMAN:	Oh, yes it is.
FATHER:	Who asked you?
SALESMAN:	I'm sorry.
FATHER:	Now, listen – just let me have a small egg, will you, please?
SALESMAN:	Certainly.

He reaches down and produces a small chocolate Easter egg.

FATHER:	That's fine. Put it in a bag.
BRICE:	Waaaaahhhhhhh!
FATHER:	Oh, keep quiet!

DISSOLVE

EXT. STREET.

SNOOKS and FATHER walk into scene. SNOOKS is admiring her egg.

BRICE:	I wanna eat the egg now, daddy.
FATHER:	Not now, Snooks. After we come out of the Museum of Art.
BRICE:	What are we going in there for?
FATHER:	You said you had to write a composition on Art, didn't you?

BRICE: Art who?

FATHER: Art nobody! Paintings, sculpture. That's Art!

BRICE: Ohhh!

FATHER: And the best place to learn about it is in the Museum. Come on – it's right over there.

BRICE: First I wanna eat my egg.

FATHER: After all that truck you've pushed into your stomach today you'll explode. Give me half of it.

BRICE: I don't wanna.

FATHER: Then just give me a little tiny piece.

BRICE: No. But I'll let you kiss me while my mouth is still gooey.

FATHER: Snooks, let me take one bit of that egg. I'm hungry. Just one bite.

BRICE: (handing him the egg)

           Awright. Just one little tiny bite.

           She watches him anxiously as he takes a huge bite out of the egg leaving just a small piece which he hands back to her.

FATHER: (mouth full) Here – you eat the rest.

BRICE: Waaaaahhhhhhh!

FATHER: What's the matter?

BRICE: Give me the bite and you take the egg!

FATHER: Please, Snooks, don't make a fuss on the street!

BRICE:	I wanna go home.
FATHER:	You wanna go home! That's a hot one! Come on – we'll go into the Museum of Art.

As they start out of scene

DISSOLVE TO

FAÇADE OF BUILDING

Museum of Art.

DISSOLVE TO

INT. MUSEUM

In the B.G. several groups of statues are behind ropes on stanchions. Visitors move along slowly. SNOOKS and FATHER come into scene. He hands her a catalog.

FATHER:	Here. This tells you all about the statues and things.
BRICE:	What is it, daddy?
FATHER:	It's a catalog. (IT'S REALLY A COPY OF THE SCRIPT IN CASE ANYBODY BLOWS ANY LINES)
BRICE:	Can I take it home with me?
FATHER:	Yes. Now don't make any noise in here. Come on.
BRICE:	Daddy.
FATHER:	What?
BRICE:	(pointing) That lady ain't got any arms!

CLOSE AND DISCREET SHOT OF THE VENUS DE MILO

TWO SHOT SNOOKS AND FATHER

FATHER: That's what happens to little girls who bite their fingernails. Let's move.

BRICE: She ain't got no clothes on.

FATHER: It's only a statue – and as a rule statues don't wear clothes.

BRICE: Why?

FATHER: Because it's considered more artistic without clothes.

BRICE: Why?

FATHER: I don't know.

BRICE: Is it like the burlesque show?

FATHER: What are you talking about?

BRICE: Well, when mummy hollered at you for going to the bur —

FATHER: Never mind that! Your mummy wouldn't know a work of art if it crawled up and bit her!

BRICE: Did they bite you at the burlesque —

FATHER: Forget about the burlesque show! I go there once just for a lark and I'm a dead pigeon the rest of my life! Now, look around and get educated!

BRICE: (still looking at Venus) She's a pretty lady, daddy. She looks just like my teacher.

FATHER: Oh, she does not!

BRICE:	How do you know?
	He glares at her. She glares back.
FATHER:	Keep your voice down.
	SNOOKS is suddenly attracted by something off to the right.
SNOOKS:	Oooh, lookit, daddy! There's Uncle Louie!
FATHER:	(looking in that direction) Where's Uncle Louie?
	CLOSE SHOT OF PITHECANTHROPUS ERECTUS (OR ANY PREHISTORIC MAN)
	BACK TO TWO SHOT SNOOKS AND FATHER
FATHER:	That's not Uncle Louie! It's a statue of the Missing Link.
BRICE:	It looks like Uncle Louie.
FATHER:	I don't care! It's the Missing Link – and it's not nice to holler out that your Uncle Louie looks like that gruesome statue.
BRICE:	(whispers) Do you think the statue heard me, daddy?
FATHER:	No. It's only a model and it's called Pithecanthropus Erectus.
BRICE:	Why?
FATHER:	That's his scientific name. Some scientists claim that men are descended from monkeys – they've discovered the Cro-Magnon man, the Neanderthal man and – and —
BRICE:	And Uncle Louie.
FATHER:	No! And several less anthropoidal species. I don't know how it works out but they fit this thing into it somehow.

BRICE:	Which thing?
FATHER:	Uncle Louie. I mean the Missing Link! That's part of evolution.
BRICE:	What's evolution, daddy?
FATHER:	I just told you. Some people believe all men were once monkeys.
BRICE:	Do you believe it?
FATHER:	It doesn't interest me.
BRICE:	Why?
FATHER:	Because I don't care if my grandfather was an ape!
BRICE:	Did your grandmother care?
FATHER:	Oh, stop it. Why aren't you making notes?
BRICE:	Notes for what, daddy?
FATHER:	For your composition. Let's sit on that bench and you can start making your notes.
	They walk a few steps and seat themselves on a bench. The bench has no back rest and SNOOKS sprawls on her stomach. Several paintings hang on the wall behind the bench.
BRICE:	This is good, daddy. We can see everything from here.
	FATHER has been searching his pockets for a notebook and pencil. As he extracts them he notices her position.
FATHER:	Sit up straight! Here – take the pencil and start writing.
	She sits cross-legged on the bench and takes pencil and book. As FATHER talks she apparently makes notes.

FATHER:	(pointing off)
	I think you might say something about that statue. It's Rodin's most famous work and it's called "Le Penseur".
BRICE:	Huh?
FATHER:	The Thinker. It's called The Thinker.
BRICE:	(laughs) That's funny, daddy.
FATHER:	What's funny about it?
BRICE:	That's what you call Uncle Louie.
FATHER:	I have never in my life called your Uncle Louie a thinker!
BRICE:	Thinker! Oh, I thought you said —
FATHER:	Never mind what you thought I said! Just write!
BRICE:	Yes, daddy.
FATHER:	(examining his catalog)
	Auguste Rodin was born in Paris in 1840 and was employed in the studio of Carriers – Belleuse where he learned to deal with the mechanical difficulties of a sculptor. In 1864 his individuality was manifested in his "Man with a Broken Nose" and he soon attained recognition and international fame thru his expert use of confluent motion in bas-relief or circular plinth eschewing contemporary methods of work. Got that?
BRICE:	Uh-huh. How do you spell work?
FATHER:	Ahh, you're not even listening to me!
BRICE:	Well, you talk too fast, daddy.
FATHER:	Just say he was a chiseller. That's good enough.

BRICE:	Let's go in that other room.
FATHER:	No – I'm too tired. Just sit still and look at the statues.
	A pretty girl walks past. FATHER follows her with appreciative eyes as she walks out of scene. SNOOKS looks at FATHER slyly.
BRICE:	Look at the statues, daddy.
FATHER:	Don't be so funny! What do you think I'm looking at?
BRICE:	I know!
FATHER:	You stop that innuendo – I'm warning you, Snooks!
BRICE:	I didn't say nothing.
FATHER:	No, but you were implying something. The reason I glanced at that girl was because her dress was torn.
BRICE:	You wasn't looking at her dress.
FATHER:	I was too – and it was torn!
BRICE:	It wasn't torn at all.
FATHER:	I say it was!
BRICE:	Oh, daddy, you were seeing things.
FATHER:	I know – but her dress was torn just the same! Put some more notes in your book.
BRICE:	(straddling bench) Maybe we should go in that other room.
FATHER:	No, that's the Egyptian room. There's nothing in there but mummies.
BRICE:	Mummy's what?

FATHER:	Just mummies!
BRICE:	Is mummy playing bridge in there?
FATHER:	No, no! These are Egyptian mummies.
BRICE:	Where do they keep their daddies?
FATHER:	This mummy has nothing to do with daddy!
BRICE:	I know. Because she caught you going to the burles —
FATHER:	Stop that! A mummy is a dried up bag of crumbling bones bound up in tight-fitting trappings.
BRICE:	I'm going to tell her what you said!
FATHER:	I'm not talking about your mummy!
BRICE:	Why?
FATHER:	And if the shoe fits she can wear it! Why don't you go look at the statues and make some notes?
BRICE:	(squirming on the floor) I wanna go home.
FATHER:	(looking at his watch) We can't go home yet. Those buzzards are still playing bridge.
BRICE:	(squirming) I wanna go home.
FATHER:	(pulling her to her feet)
	Please, Snooks. Don't make a scene in here. Come on, let's enjoy these wonderful paintings then we can get out of this broken-down place.
	They turn to the paintings behind them.
BRICE:	(turning away) I don't wanna see no paintings. I wanna go home!

FATHER:	Shh! Please, Snooks... Oh, look at this gorgeous thing. Leda and the Swan!
BRICE:	Where?
FATHER:	This one. Isn't it beautiful?
BRICE:	Yeah. Can I touch it?
FATHER:	No, you can't touch it. Why would you want to touch it?
BRICE:	I wanna see if the swan's got real fur on it?
FATHER:	It's not fur silly. Swans don't have fur, they have down. His whole coat is down.
BRICE:	Huh?
FATHER:	I said that swan's whole coat is down.
BRICE:	Is his pants down, too?
FATHER:	Keep moving, Snooks. It'll soon be time to go home.

They move along to the next picture.

BRICE:	What's that one, daddy? With the old lady in a chair.
FATHER:	It's called "A Study in Black and White". That's a Whistler.
BRICE:	I wanna hear it whistle.
FATHER:	It can't whistle.
BRICE:	I wanna hear it whistle.
FATHER:	That's the artist's name – Whistler! Oh, look at this gigantic mural!

SHOT OF A LARGE MURAL PAINTED TO CONFORM WITH THE ENSUING DESCRIPTION.

BRICE'S VOICE: That's a big one, isn't it, daddy?

FATHER'S VOICE:

It's a masterpiece. That's the celebrated "Circus Maximus" by Corot. It says there.

TWO SHOT SNOOKS AND FATHER

As they stare intently at the picture which is not visible now.

BRICE: What's them lions doing?

FATHER: (gives a surreptitious glance at his catalog)

Well, that was a sport that the cruel Roman emperors used to indulge in. First they'd be entertained by the gladiators who fought and wrestled until one or the other was killed.

SNOOKS makes a pained expression.

FATHER: Even that gory amusement wasn't enough to appease the blood-thirsty appetites of the barbarous rulers, so they'd turn loose ten or twelve of the most ferocious and hungry lions they could find – and then – into this huge arena with those loose lions they'd push some poor, innocent citizens.

SNOOKS: (really looking worried) Uh-huh.

FATHER: This painting depicts the ancient savagery in all its horrible cruelty. The grinning, hideous faces of the spectators, the ravenous, yawning jaws of the hungry lions and the plight of the poor innocents about to be devoured.

BRICE:	(breaks down) Waaaaahhhhhh!
FATHER:	Oh, I'm so sorry, Snooks. I didn't think you'd be so touched.
BRICE:	(crying) It's awful, daddy.
FATHER:	I'm gratified that you're able to see evil in such fierce lust.
BRICE:	That's not why I'm crying.
FATHER:	It's not? Then what are you crying about?
BRICE:	(pointing) That little lion in the corner ain't getting any!
FATHER:	(disgusted) Ahhh – what's the use – come on home!

He starts dragging her out of the scene as we

FADE OUT

Playing Hooking
(April 13, 1939)

MAXWELL HOUSE (REVISED)

4-13-39

YOUNG: And now, ladies and gentlemen, here is Fanny Brice as Baby Snooks!

(MUSIC...APPLAUSE)

YOUNG: Daddy, played by Hanley Stafford, has decided to give Snooks another chance in public school before hiring a special tutor. As the scene opens he is waiting for her to come home – hoping that all has gone well. Listen.

FATHER: (SINGS) Schooldays, schooldays, dear old Golden Rule days – Hmm hmm hmm --- (DOORBELL RINGS) Oh, that must be my baby! (CALLS) I'm coming, Snooks!

(DOOR OPENS AND CLOSES)

BRICE: Hello, daddy.

FATHER: Hello, darling. Well, how was school today?

BRICE: Fine.

FATHER: Good! Come in here, Snooks.

BRICE: Why?

FATHER:	Well, I've laid out a little homework for you to do. It'll help you get ahead in school.
BRICE:	(Laughs) I wanna go out and play.
FATHER:	Oh, it'll only take a minute. Now here – I've written down two sentences. You read them.
BRICE:	Mmm hmm. (READS) The hen has four leg.... Who done it?
FATHER:	Good. Now, what's wrong with them?
BRICE:	Huh?
FATHER:	What's wrong with these sentences?.... The hen has four legs. Who done it?
BRICE:	He didn't done it – the angels done it.
FATHER:	No, no. It should be he *did* it!
BRICE:	How did he do it, daddy?
FATHER:	Do what?
BRICE:	Get four legs?
FATHER:	They don't have four legs.
BRICE:	Horsies is got four legs.
FATHER:	Oh, nobody's got four legs!
FATHER:	I'm talking about a hen! No hen has four legs!
BRICE:	Why?
FATHER:	Oh forget it. We'll do the homework some other time. Go out and play.
BRICE:	Awight.

FATHER:	Oh wait a minute – I gave you a quarter this morning to get some exercise books. Did you buy them?
BRICE:	Huh?
FATHER:	Did you buy those books with the quarter I gave you?
BRICE:	No, daddy. The money fell down the sewer.
FATHER:	Snooks! Look at me! Are you sure you didn't spend that money on candy?
BRICE:	No, daddy.
FATHER:	Then what's that on your face?
BRICE:	It's my nose.
FATHER:	No, I mean around your mouth. That's chocolate! How did it get there?
BRICE:	Er – I fell down and there was chocolate on the sidewalk.
FATHER:	There's something fishy about this. Now I'm going to find (PHONE RINGS) Hello, yes – this is Mr. Higgins…Oh, Miss Grub. Oh yes, my daughter's teacher. Oh, what – why… Of course – I sent her back to school this morning!
BRICE:	I think I'll go now.
FATHER:	Stay here, you!… Hello Hello…Yes…Oh, she didn't eh? Thank you, Miss Grub. I'll attend to her. Goodbye… (HANGS UP)…So!
BRICE:	Ohhhhh!

FATHER: Well, Snooks – I don't intend to mince words with you this time! You haven't been in school today. Have you?

BRICE: Huh?

FATHER: Now don't stall! I know you played hooky!

BRICE: Who told you?

FATHER: A little birdie told me!

BRICE: Was the birdie's name Miss Grub?

FATHER: (MIMICS HER) Yes, the birdie's name was Miss Grub!

BRICE: Don't believe her, daddy – she's a bigger liar than me.

FATHER: Out with it! Why didn't you go to school?

BRICE: I did go, daddy.

FATHER: I thought it was kind of funny – coming home so early! It's an hour earlier than usual.

BRICE: Is it?

FATHER: Yes! Now why are you home so soon?

BRICE: Er - they let us go home early because –

FATHER: Because what?

BRICE: 'Cause teacher got a new baby today.

FATHER: Snooks! Your teacher's not even married!

BRICE: She's gonna get married tomorrow.

FATHER: Tomorrow!

BRICE: That's why they let us go home, daddy. And I don't have to go for two more days.

FATHER:	Why not?
BRICE:	She had triplets.
FATHER:	Oh – now – You've got to confess that you didn't go to school!
BRICE:	Why?
FATHER:	Because I know you didn't. Oh don't you see, Snooks – all I want is the truth. I promise you I won't lose my temper if you tell me the truth.
BRICE:	Awight. I'll tell the truth.
FATHER:	Well, go ahead.
BRICE:	What will you do to me if I played hooky?
FATHER:	I'll give you the licking of your life!
BRICE:	(QUICKLY) I went to school!
FATHER:	Now Snooks, do you remember you promised never to play hooky again?
BRICE:	Uh-huh.
FATHER:	And I promised if you did play hooky – I'd give you a spanking!
BRICE:	Uh-huh!
FATHER:	Well?
BRICE:	Well, I didn't keep my promise so you don't have to keep yours.
FATHER:	Then you do admit you didn't go to school today!
BRICE:	I tried to go, daddy – but I couldn't.

FATHER: Oh, why not?

BRICE: 'Cause three eagles wouldn't let me.

FATHER: What three eagles?

BRICE: What did you say, daddy?

FATHER: You said three eagles wouldn't let you go to school!

(OMONOUSLY) Well - I'm waiting!

BRICE: I'm thinkin', daddy.

FATHER: Oh! Brother, this is the best one yet!

BRICE: You like it, daddy?

FATHER: No – I don't like it! Now what about those three eagles?

BRICE: Just as I was going into the school they chased me away.

FATHER: Oh stop it! You can't make me believe any excuse about three eagles, Snooks!

BRICE: Oh. Will you believe it about *two* eagles?

FATHER: No!

BRICE: One eagle?

FATHER: I won't believe it about any eagles!

BRICE: Don't you like eagles, daddy?

FATHER: Now Snooks! How dare you tell me an eagle stopped you from going to school! Why there isn't an eagle in this whole part of the country!

BRICE: Well, it was an awful big sparrow.

FATHER: Snooks! I've had enough of this.

BRICE:	Me too – goodbye, daddy!
FATHER:	Now stay! I'm not thru with you. I want you to tell me the truth – you understand? The truth!
BRICE:	Awight, daddy.
FATHER:	Now, why didn't you go to school?
BRICE:	A lion ran after me and chased me right into a candy store.
FATHER:	Oh – a lion! And where did the lion come from?
BRICE:	From the circus.
FATHER:	Circus! There isn't a circus here.
BRICE:	Yes there is – I seen the posters.
FATHER:	Oh those posters were left over from last year!
BRICE:	So was the lion, daddy.
FATHER:	All right! So a lion chased you into the candy store!
BRICE:	You believe it?
FATHER:	Oh, sure! I believe that eagle stuff, too!
BRICE:	Then why are you taking off your slipper?
FATHER:	Because there's a kangaroo in my toe! (ANGRY LAUGH)
BRICE:	(LAUGHS) Waaahhh!
FATHER:	Now stop yelling and go on with your fantastic story. What did you do when the lion chased you into a candy store?

BRICE:	I had an ice-cream soda.
FATHER:	So that's where the quarter went!
BRICE:	(FAST) But I didn't drink it.
FATHER:	Why not?
BRICE:	'Cause four more lions jumped on me daddy.
FATHER:	And then what happened?
BRICE:	I got killed.
FATHER:	What am I going to do with you, Snooks?
BRICE:	Kiss me, daddy.
FATHER:	How could you tell me such stories about lions? Why you know you never even saw a lion!
BRICE:	Yes I did, daddy.
FATHER:	Where did you see a lion?
BRICE:	The lady next door has one – and that's the one that chased me.
FATHER:	The lady next door has a lion?
BRICE:	Mm-hmm.
FATHER:	Snooks, you know very well that's nothing but a little yellow dog.
BRICE:	It looks like a lion.
FATHER:	Now I want you to kneel down this instant and pray for forgiveness for telling so many fibs!
BRICE:	Awight, daddy.

FATHER:	Now get down now. Now pray to heaven to make you an honest child. (TO HIMSELF) Never heard such a thing! Three eagles and four lions! Oh!
BRICE:	I'm finished, daddy!
FATHER:	Did you pray?
BRICE:	Uh-huh. And the angel said, "I forgive you Snooks. The first time I looked at that yellow dog, I thought he was a lion, too."
FATHER:	I give up!

(MUSIC...APPLAUSE)

Daddy Buys Snook a Stove
(April 20, 1939)

MAXWELL HOUSE COFFEE TIME

April 20, 1939

YOUNG: And Now, Ladies and Gentlemen, Here is Fanny Brice as Baby Snooks!

(MUSIC)... APPLAUSE

YOUNG: Well, today is Snooks' birthday. As the scene opens, Daddy, played by Hanley Stafford, is taking her to the toy shop to buy her a little present.....Listen.

FATHER: Well, Snooks, we'll be at the toy store in just a minute. Have you made up your mind what you want?

BRICE: Uh-huh.

FATHER: What do you want?

BRICE: The whole store.

FATHER: Don't be silly – You can't have the whole store!

BRICE: Why?

FATHER: Because I'm not that rich!

BRICE: Is you poor, Daddy?

FATHER:	No. I'm just as you might say – half and half.
BRICE:	(LAUGHS) Then buy me half the store.
FATHER:	Now look, Snooks – Let's have it understood before we go in. I don't want you going around saying "I want this and I want that and I want the other thing."
BRICE:	Then how will I get it?
FATHER:	Get what?
BRICE:	The whole store.
FATHER:	Oh stop that! I told you I won't buy you the whole store!
BRICE:	Why?
FATHER:	Because I can't afford it! And I positively refuse to spend a lot of money on useless things.
BRICE:	Waaahhh!
FATHER:	What are you crying about?
BRICE:	You do it for mommy.
FATHER:	Never mind that! Now I'll buy you one or two toys but I don't want to get things that will annoy me. No mechanical toys that I have to keep winding!
BRICE:	Will you buy me a drum?
FATHER:	If I do you'll keep disturbing me when I'm working.
BRICE:	No I won't, Daddy – I'll only drum when you're asleep.
FATHER:	Forget the drum. Now get a useful toy – like a little electric stove. You might learn how to cook.
BRICE:	Is that useful, Daddy?

FATHER:	Why, of course. Everybody should know how to cook.
BRICE:	Why?
FATHER:	Oh, come on – Here's the toy shop. Let's go in – and remember, Snooks – a little electric stove and that's all.
BRICE:	Awight, Daddy.
	(DOOR OPENS AND CLOSES)
FATHER:	Here's the saleslady. Now just behave, Snooks.
BRICE:	Mm-hmm.
WOMAN:	Yes sir? Oh hello, little girl – what can I do for you?
BRICE:	Daddy wants an electric stove.
WOMAN:	Don't you want it?
BRICE:	No – I want a drum!
FATHER:	Now listen, Snooks – we agreed on a stove and that's what you're going to get. Miss, will you please show her the stove?
WOMAN:	Yes, we have a full line of cooking toys right over here. Now, what kind of a stove would you like, little girl?
BRICE:	(LAUGHS) A stove with a drum on top.
FATHER:	Snooks!
WOMAN:	Say – here's a little beauty! If you put the plug in the socket it actually works.
BRICE:	Ohhhhh – I like it!
WOMAN:	You really like it?

BRICE:	Uh-huh.
WOMAN:	Shall I pack it up?
BRICE:	No.
WOMAN:	Why not?
BRICE:	It ain't got a drum.
FATHER:	Snooks, there is no such thing as a stove with a drum! You can have a stove without the drum.
BRICE:	Can have a drum without a stove?
FATHER:	No!
BRICE:	Why?
FATHER:	Because you can't! I told you I want to get something useful. Now, pick out a stove.
BRICE:	I can't cook, Daddy.
FATHER:	Well, look I - I'll be glad to play with the little stove and teach you how to cook.
BRICE:	Is you gonna play with it?
FATHER:	Well, just to teach you.
BRICE:	You did that with my washing machine and you broke it!
FATHER:	I didn't break it - Grandpa did!
BRICE:	You was both playing with it all day!
FATHER:	We were not! And Snooks, you know very well when your washing machine broke, I bought you a bicycle to make up for it!
BRICE:	I could never get on it!

FATHER:	Well, why not?
BRICE:	'Cause you was riding it all the time!
FATHER:	Oh, nonsense! It was altogether too small for me to ride on.
BRICE:	Mmmm, that's why it busted!
FATHER:	Oh, never mind all this! Pick out the stove you want and let's go home!
BRICE:	Awight, daddy.
WOMAN:	Oh here - look at this. All chromium fitted and the pots and pans go with it!
BRICE:	Ohhh - I like it!
WOMAN:	Oh fine! Is it big enough?
BRICE:	Uh-huh.
FATHER:	Shall we take it with us?
BRICE:	NO!
FATHER:	Why not!
BRICE:	It ain't got a drum!
FATHER:	All right - that's enough! Miss, pack up that little stove for the child.
BRICE:	Waaaaahhh!
FATHER:	Oh please, Snooks, please, now be sensible. Here - I'll buy you some more toys if you'll behave. Oh miss! Pack in that chemical set - that toy dynamo and erector - and that carpenter's tool box! Is there anything else you'd like, Snooks?

BRICE:	Uh-huh.
FATHER:	Well, what is it?
BRICE:	Something I can play with!
	(MUSIC....APPLAUSE)

Part 2

YOUNG:	Here she is again, ladies and gentlemen - Baby Snooks! Daddy and Snooks have just arrived home and he's ready to give his child her first cooking lesson. Now here they are!
	(MUSIC)
FATHER:	All right, Snooks. What do you want to cook?
BRICE:	Ice cream.
FATHER:	Oh, don't be silly - you can't make ice cream on a stove!
BRICE:	Why?
FATHER:	You don't cook ice cream - you freeze it! That's the difference between hot and cold.
BRICE:	What is?
FATHER:	Didn't you ever get burned?
BRICE:	Uh-huh.
FATHER:	Did you ever go out in a cold frost and your ears got very red? Weren't they cold?

BRICE:	No - they burned!
FATHER:	Well, of course, when a thing is extremely cold - it produces a burn like that of heat, and heat is also used to freeze by burning in surgery so that when you apply ice it burns and vice versa!
BRICE:	Do you feel all right, daddy?
FATHER:	I feel fine, Snooks! Now, what would you like to cook?
BRICE:	Ice cream!
FATHER:	Now, don't start that again! You can't make ice cream on a stove!
BRICE:	Why?
FATHER:	Because you can't! Here - I've got Mummy's cookbook and we'll pick out a nice easy recipe that you can make.
BRICE:	What's a recipe?
FATHER:	A recipe tells you how to cook things.
BRICE:	Is there one for ice cream?
FATHER:	Of course.
BRICE:	Oh, so you can cook it!
FATHER:	*No you can't cook ice cream!*
BRICE:	Why?
FATHER:	Ohhh! And some people even adopt them!
BRICE:	Huh?
FATHER:	Now look, now here's a recipe - how to make fish cakes!

BRICE:	How, daddy?
FATHER:	Let me read it… Take one fish ---
BRICE:	I'll get the goldfish, daddy!
FATHER:	No, no! It must be an ordinary fish! You take out all the bones and chop it up!
BRICE:	Chop up the bones?
FATHER:	No - chop up the fish.
BRICE:	What fish?
FATHER:	Any fish!
BRICE:	A goldfish?
FATHER:	Any fish but a gold fish!
BRICE:	A whale?
FATHER:	Snooks - people don't eat whales and they don't eat goldfish!
BRICE:	Does whales eat goldfish?
FATHER:	I don't know - Yes! Whales eat all little fish.
BRICE:	Sardines?
FATHER:	Yes!
SNOOKS:	How do they open the cans?
FATHER:	I don't know! Let's start cooking something. Now here's a piece of fish in the ice box. I'll get the stove plugged in and you wash the fish.
BRICE:	Why?

FATHER:	To make it clean.
BRICE:	(LAUGHS)
FATHER:	Well, what are you laughing at? What are you laughing at?
BRICE:	I dunno.
FATHER:	Come on, wash it and make it very clean, while I go get some flour.
BRICE:	Awight! I'll make it very clean, daddy. (WATER SPLASHING)
BRICE:	(SINGS) Fishy, fishy, in the brook, daddy catch him on a hook, mummy fry him in the pan ---
FATHER:	Well, have you washed it, Snooks?
BRICE:	Uh-huh!
FATHER:	All right now, we'll put it through the grinder... like that... (EFFECT OF GRINDER)
BRICE:	(LAUGHS)
FATHER:	We'll roll it in the flour like that and -
BRICE:	(LAUGHS)
FATHER:	You'll fry it on your little stove.
BRICE:	Awight! Shall I put it in the pan?
FATHER:	Yes...Now while the fishcake is frying we can make spaghetti.
BRICE:	What's spaghetti?
FATHER:	Well, it's a food created by the Italians.

BRICE:	What's Italians?
FATHER:	Italians are people who speak Italian.
BRICE:	Could I talk Italian?
FATHER:	Why, of course not - it's not your language. You can't speak a word of it.
BRICE:	Well, how do Italians understand it?
FATHER:	It's their language.
BRICE:	Do you speak Italian?
FATHER:	Yes - I can speak Italian.
BRICE:	Then why don't you speak it?
FATHER:	Because it's a different language!
BRICE:	What's a different language?
FATHER:	Italian! Italian is the language of the people who created spaghetti. Is that clear?
BRICE:	Uh-huh.
FATHER:	Now let's make some spaghetti.
BRICE:	What's spaghetti?
FATHER:	Listen, Snooks - spaghetti is long stringy dough rolled into thin tubes that are dried out in the sun until they crisp and do you know who invented this dish?
BRICE:	Huh?
FATHER:	Who invented spaghetti?
BRICE:	Waaaahhh!

FATHER:	What are you crying for?
BRICE:	I didn't do it!
FATHER:	Good heavens, the fish cake nearly burned!
BRICE:	Oh!
FATHER:	Here, let me take it off the stove. Oh now, aren't you proud that you learned how to make a fish cake? Doesn't it look good?
BRICE:	No!
FATHER:	Why, I think it looks wonderful.
BRICE:	Then why don't you eat it?
FATHER:	All right - serve it to me on that little plate and I'll be glad to eat it.
BRICE:	Awight - here it is!
FATHER:	Very well. (EATS) Good heavens - this tastes awful. Snooks, did you wash this fish?
BRICE:	Uh-huh! And I made it very clean, daddy.
FATHER:	What do you mean?
BRICE:	I washed it with soap!
FATHER:	Soap! (SLAP)
BRICE:	Waaah!!
	(MUSIC......APPLAUSE)

At the Dentist

FANNY BRICE-BABY SNOOKS

(Dentist Spot)

SOUND	(DOOR BELL...DOOR OPENS AND CLOSES)
FATHER	How do you do? Is the dentist in?
NURSE	Yes, Mr. Higgins. Just be seated and Dr. Hoyt will see Baby Snooks in a minute.
FATHER	Thank you...come here, Snooks. Sit right here next to daddy.
BRICE	Alright.
FATHER	Now look, Snooks, this is the fifth time I've brought you to the dentist, and each time we come you forget which tooth hurts you. This time you've got to be absolutely sure. Now, which tooth hurts?
BRICE	It don't hurt now.
FATHER	There you go again. Every time I bring you to the dentist's office you say it stops hurting. Why is that?
BRICE	It only hurts when I eat candy.
FATHER	Well here's a piece of chocolate. Chew it and tell me which tooth hurts

BRICE	Alright...mmmmmmmmmmmmmmm....it's good candy.
FATHER	Never mind that. Which tooth hurts?
BRICE	It don't hurt.
FATHER	But you told me if you chewed candy it would hurt you.
BRICE	I swallowed it too quick.
FATHER	Well try another piece...
BRICE	Alright...MMMMmmm...this is better than the other one!
FATHER	Listen, I'm not asking you for an opinion about the candy. I want to know which tooth hurts.
BRICE	Give me another piece of candy and I'll find out.
FATHER	Here you are. This is the very last piece of chocolate. It's the last piece, understand? Now chew it slowly.
BRICE	Alright...Mmmm... (CRIES) Waaaaaaaaaahh!!
FATHER	Ah, that's good! Did you find the tooth that hurts you?
BRICE	No!
FATHER	Then what are you crying about?
BRICE	I want more candy!
FATHER	Do you realize you ate a whole bar of chocolate and you didn't find out which tooth hurts? Why is that?

BRICE	Because I just remembered.
FATHER	Remembered what?
BRICE	It only hurts with ice cream.
FATHER	Now stop stalling, Snooks. You've got to have the tooth out and you have no reason to be afraid. Doctor Hoyt is a very fine dentist and never hurts anybody.
SOUND	(LOUD PROLONGED GROAN FROM DENTIST'S OFFICE)
BRICE	(FRIGHTENED) Oooooh, daddy, what's that?
FATHER	Doctor Hoyt is working on a patient inside.
BRICE	With a hatchet?
FATHER	No-no. Doctor Hoyt never hurts anybody.
SOUND	(ANOTHER GROAN)
BRICE	Daddy—I wanna go home.
NURSE	Will you step this way? Doctor Hoyt will see you now.
FATHER	Thank you, nurse. Come on, Snooks.
SOUND	(DOOR SLAM)
DENTIST	Ah, my little girl—sit right here on this nice big chair.
BRICE	(SCARED) Oh, daddy.
FATHER	Don't be afraid, darling. I'll hold your hand.
BRICE	Hold the dentist's hand!
DENTIST	Now, now...my dear child, you have nothing to be afraid of. I'm painless.

BRICE	But I ain't.
DENTIST	Now open your mouth and I'll just touch the tooth with my finger.
BRICE	Alright.
DENTIST	Ow! You hurt me! Why did you bite my finger?
BRICE	I thought you was painless!
DENTIST	Now when I touch your tooth, tell me if it hurts. Does this one hurt?
BRICE	(FRIGHTENED) Uh-huh.
DENTIST	And this one?
BRICE	(FRIGHTENED) Uh-huh.
DENTIST	This one too?
BRICE	(FRIGHTENED) Uh-huh.
DENTIST	All your teeth hurt?
BRICE	Uh-huh and my feet too!
DENTIST	Your feet too?
BRICE	Yeah...I hurt all over! (CRIES) I wanna go home!
DENTIST	Now don't be nervous. It's that little tooth in the back. I'll take it out in a jiffy.
BRICE	And will you put it back?
DENTIST	No...once you take a tooth out you can't put it back.
BRICE	Why?
DENTIST	Well you just can't do it.

BRICE	Well I want you to put it back.
FATHER	Stop that nonsense, Snooks. You can't put your teeth back!
BRICE	(CRIES) Waaaaaaaaaahhhhhhhh!
FATHER	What are you crying about?
BRICE	Uncle Louie does it. Puts his teeth back.
DENTIST	Now little girl, just close your eyes and open your mouth.
BRICE	I don't wanna.
DENTIST	I'm not going to do anything to you.
BRICE	What have you got behind your back?
DENTIST	Nothing at all.
BRICE	I know what it is.
DENTIST	What is it?
BRICE	The hatchet you killed the man with!
FATHER	Snooks, stop carrying on. You ought to be ashamed of yourself. Why, I've had teeth pulled and I was never afraid. I never made a sound.
BRICE	Let me see you.
FATHER	Well, I have no tooth that bothers me. But just to show you, I'll sit in that chair and let the dentist do anything he likes.
DENTIST	That's a good idea, Mr. Higgins. It will give the child confidence.

FATHER	Very well. Let me sit in the chair, Snooks.
BRICE	Alright.
FATHER	You see how I open my mouth without any trouble?
BRICE	And if he pulls your tooth you wouldn't holler?
FATHER	Certainly not.
BRICE	Well, let me see him do it!
FATHER	But I have no tooth that needs to be pulled. Have I, Doctor?
DENTIST	Well, Mr. Higgins, there is one tooth that might come out!
FATHER	What's that?
DENTIST	Yes—you're better off with that back tooth out.
BRICE	Don't be afraid, daddy—I'll hold your hand.
FATHER	Wait a minute—this is ridiculous! That tooth doesn't hurt me!
BRICE	Well, mine don't hurt me!
FATHER	But yours has a cavity!
BRICE	So has yours!
FATHER	I'll stand for no more nonsense! Snooks, get back in that chair. Now open your mouth–quick!
BRICE	(STARTING TO CRY) Alright, daddy.
DENTIST	Now, one—two—three!
BRICE	(YELLS) Woowww!!!

DENTIST	Now, there you are—it's out! Doesn't it feel better?
BRICE	You pulled the wrong tooth!
FATHER	Snooks, what do you mean he pulled the wrong tooth? Where's the tooth that hurts you?
BRICE	In my pocket!
FATHER	In your pocket?
BRICE	Yeah—it fell out this morning!

(APPLAUSE)

(MUSIC PLAYOFF)

Golfing

MAXWELL HOUSE
5-18-39 (REVISED)

YOUNG: And now, Ladies and Gentlemen, here is Fanny Brice as Baby Snooks!

(MUSIC …. APPLAUSE)

YOUNG: Daddy, played by Hanley Stafford, has a golf appointment with his boss this morning and he's promised to meet him on the golf course rain or shine. As our scene opens, Daddy's alarm clock is calling insistently.

(ALARM RINGS THREE TIMES)

FATHER: (YAWNS) Hmmm... Okay... Okay. Oh boy, am I tired!

BRICE: Hello, daddy. Here–I made you some coffee!

FATHER: Coffee? Huh? It looks like plain water to me.

BRICE: Make believe, daddy. Make believe it's coffee.

FATHER: All right it–it's coffee.

BRICE: Drink it.

FATHER: Okay. (DRINKS) Mmm–well that's wonderful coffee, Snooks.

BRICE: You like it? I'll make some more.

FATHER: No–don't go to any more trouble, Snooks.

BRICE: It ain't no trouble, daddy–I got it from the goldfish bowl.

FATHER: Eh, what!

BRICE: Ain't it good coffee?

FATHER: Oh, what's the matter with you, Snooks? Is that all you could think of to give me for breakfast–water from the goldfish bowl!

BRICE: I was only playin' house, daddy.

FATHER: Well that's no way to play! No child makes her father drink the water from a goldfish bowl!

BRICE: I did.

FATHER: Now don't get smart! Snooks, I'd just like to go for one whole day without giving you a spanking!

BRICE: Awight, daddy. I'll let you.

FATHER: Ahhh! Go back to bed.

BRICE: Why?

FATHER: Because it's too early for you to be up.

BRICE: Why are you up?

FATHER: Well, I have a golf appointment and I've got to hurry.

BRICE: Will you read me the funnies?

FATHER: No! I haven't got time.

BRICE: Why?

FATHER:	Because I'm going to play golf!
BRICE:	Who with, daddy?
FATHER:	With my boss. And it's very important that I be there on time! He gets very mad if I'm late.
BRICE:	Who does?
FATHER:	My boss!
BRICE:	Who's he?
FATHER:	He's the man I work for! Get out of my way–I've got to hurry and wash!
BRICE:	No, read me the funnies.
FATHER:	No! Now go back to bed this instant!
BRICE:	If you don't read me the funnies, your boss is gonna be mad.
FATHER:	Well, why should my boss be mad?
BRICE:	'Cause you'll be late.
FATHER:	Snooks! Who teaches you these wonderful tricks?
BRICE:	Nobody–I make 'em up. (LAUGHS)
FATHER:	Oho! You're looking for a spanking this morning!
BRICE:	Oho! Read me the funnies.
FATHER:	I will not! Now if you waste another second of my time, I'll tan you good! Now stay out of the bathroom till I get thru.
BRICE:	What you gonna do, daddy?

FATHER:	I'm going to shave–and I don't want you bothering me!
BRICE:	Why?
FATHER:	Because I'm late already. I should have left ten minutes ago.
BRICE:	Where you going?
FATHER:	To play golf!
BRICE:	Who with?
FATHER:	I told you–with my boss!
BRICE:	Who's he?
FATHER:	Snooks–if you ask me one more question I–I'll jump in the bathtub and drown myself!
BRICE:	Let me run the water, daddy!
FATHER:	Ohhh! And they think they've got trouble in Europe!
BRICE:	Huh?
FATHER:	Nothing! Get out of here and let me shave!
BRICE:	I wanna watch.
FATHER:	(CRIES FOR HER BENEFIT) Oh, Snooks–how can you be so nasty to your poor old daddy. I work like a slave to see that you have everything and you won't let me have just a little fun. (PROP SOBS)
BRICE:	(LAUGHS)
FATHER:	Well what's so funny about it?
BRICE:	You sound like mummy.

FATHER: Well never mind that!

BRICE: (LAUGHS)

FATHER: Mummy's up in the country enjoying herself while I'm–holy smoke! You want to do something for daddy, Snooks?

BRICE: What's the matter daddy?

FATHER: Mummy called last night and told me to order a bathing suit for her. I'll be on the golf course so you call the store as soon as it opens.

BRICE: Awight.

FATHER: Now, listen carefully. Order a bathing suit–large girl's size–salmon color–fastened by one large pearl button with two little holes in it. Can you remember that?

BRICE: Uh-huh.

FATHER: Have it charged to me. Just tell them who I am and it'll be all right. Now, what are you going to say?

BRICE: I want a large bathing suit for a girl fastened in it with a pearl salmon. Just tell me who I am and I'll be all right.

FATHER: Not pearl salmon! Button.

BRICE: Huh?

FATHER: Button–button!

BRICE: Button, button, who's got the button. Let's play, daddy.

FATHER: I have no time to play. Will you order that suit?

BRICE: What suit?

FATHER:	What did I just ask you to do?
BRICE:	Er–you want a large swimming hole with a pearl colored girl and two salmons in it.
FATHER:	No! No!
BRICE:	A little swimming suit for a large salmon?
FATHER:	What are you talking about?
BRICE:	For a girl with no buttons.
FATHER:	Ahh–forget it! If she wants to swim let her wear an apron! Well I've got to finish shaving! Oh brother–I'll never make it!
BRICE:	Make what, daddy?
FATHER:	My appointment!
BRICE:	Where you going?
FATHER:	I told you fifty times! To play golf!
BRICE:	Who with?
FATHER:	My boss!
BRICE:	Who's he?
FATHER:	The man I work for!
BRICE:	Ohhhh! I wanna go with you.
FATHER:	No! You can't go with me!
BRICE:	Why?
FATHER:	Because you'd drive me crazy on a golf course.
BRICE:	Then read me the funnies!

FATHER:	No! Look out–I'm gonna get my clubs and get out of here fast! … Hmmm–where are my clubs? Well I know I left them in this closet!
BRICE:	I think I'll go to bed now.
FATHER:	Snooks! You wait a minute–where are my golf clubs?
BRICE:	If I tell you will you take me with you?
FATHER:	No!
BRICE:	Then I don't know where they are–goodbye!
FATHER:	Come here! All right–tell me where they are and I'll take you.
BRICE:	You promise, daddy?
FATHER:	Yes! I promise! Where are my clubs?
BRICE:	I gave them to the junkman yesterday!
FATHER:	What for?
BRICE:	For a stack of funny papers! (LAUGHS)
FATHER:	You little–(SLAP)
BRICE:	WAAHHHHHH!
	(MUSIC …… APPLAUSE)
YOUNG:	Don't leave, folks! Baby Snooks and daddy will be back later on in the program and you'll meet them on the golf course. I can just imagine what's going to happen to daddy's game! Stand by and get the results.
YOUNG:	Here she is again, Ladies and Gentlemen! Baby Snooks on the golf course! She is standing on the first tee with daddy, who seems to be in a murderous mood!

(MUSIC)

FATHER: Cost me two dollars to rent these broken-down clubs and then I find the boss didn't wait for me! I'll probably get fired, too! Come on–let's get out of here.

BRICE: Ain't you gonna play golf, daddy?

FATHER: No! No use going out without–oh–wait a minute. I might as well play nine holes. I've paid my green fees and rented the clubs. But I'll play only on one condition, Snooks. You must remain absolutely quiet when I go to hit the ball!

BRICE: I promise, daddy.

FATHER: All right. Let me get a ball out of the bag.

BRICE: Here's one, daddy.

FATHER: Where'd you get that, Snooks?

BRICE: I found it when we was walking over here.

FATHER: Oh. Are you sure it was lost?

BRICE: Uh-huh–I seen the man lookin' for it.

FATHER: Oh, well. I'll turn it in later. Stand back–I want to take a practice swing with this driver… (SWISH) … -uh- not bad, huh? How do you like my form, Snooks?

BRICE: I think you're very pretty, daddy.

FATHER: All right–Now I'm going to start. Now don't get too close.

BRICE: What you doing?

FATHER: I'm putting the ball on the tee.

BRICE:	Is that tea? It looks like dirt.
FATHER:	It is dirt.
BRICE:	You said it was tea.
FATHER:	I know I did! But this tee isn't the same as the tea you drink.
BRICE:	Why?
FATHER:	Because one is a beverage and the other is ground!
BRICE:	I thought coffee was ground.
FATHER:	Coffee is ground! But this is a different tee and a different ground! Does that answer your question?
BRICE:	I didn't ask you nothin'.
FATHER:	Well, don't! Now keep quiet and let me hit the ball.
BRICE:	Awight …… daddy?
FATHER:	What is it?
BRICE:	Where you gonna hit it to?
FATHER:	You see that flag way down there?
BRICE:	Is today a holiday?
FATHER:	No! Today is not a holiday!
BRICE:	Then why have they got all the flags here?
FATHER:	Those flags indicate the position of the green!
BRICE:	What green?
FATHER:	Where the hole is! Wherever you see a flag there's a hole!

BRICE:	Well why don't they fix it?
FATHER:	Fix what?
BRICE:	The hole in the flag.
FATHER:	The flag hasn't got a hole in it! The green has a hole in it!
BRICE:	Why?
FATHER:	So I can crawl in and pull it over my head! (MAD LAUGH)
BRICE:	(LAUGHS) WAAAAHHH!
FATHER:	Now stop that yelling! Now move back a little–and don't make a sound! You just watch the ball when I hit it.
BRICE:	Awight, daddy.
FATHER:	Now! Head down–right hand over–bring the club–back–slowly––
BRICE:	Daddy!
FATHER:	Ohhh! What is it now?
BRICE:	Why don't you hit the ball?
FATHER:	That's what I'm trying to do!
BRICE:	Then why are you puttin' the stick around your neck?
FATHER:	Oh. Leave me alone! How will I ever shoot a par?
BRICE:	Huh?
FATHER:	I'm trying to shoot a par!
BRICE:	Whose pa you gonna shoot, daddy?

FATHER: Nobody's pa! I said par–not pa! The object of the game is to shoot par!

BRICE: Why don't you shoot ma, daddy?

FATHER: Now don't give me ideas!

BRICE: Huh?

FATHER: Nothing! Now just let me drive off this first tee, will you? The people are all staring at us.

BRICE: Awight.

FATHER: Now don't make a sound. Here I go. Knees bent–left shoulder down–eye on the ball–(GRUNT AND SWISH OF CLUB).

BRICE: You missed it, daddy!

FATHER: Uh. Tough course! …… Well I guess this rented driver is no good. Oh I wish I had a brassie.

BRICE: Why?

FATHER: Well this cheap outfit only has five sticks. I usually carry ten.

BRICE: Why?

FATHER: Because I need them. Hagen has about twenty, Alex Morrison has twenty-four, Charley Lacey has twenty-six–and–

BRICE: And all the rest have thirty-one except February which has twenty-eight! Ain't I smart, daddy? (LAUGHS)

FATHER:	Yeah, you're very smart! Now, keep quiet for two minutes and let me hit this ball! Now stand back! Eye on the ball–firm grip–right hand over–come back slowly–(SLIGHT PAUSE)–well, go ahead and talk if you're going to!
BRICE:	I ain't gonna talk, daddy.
FATHER:	Okay! Back slowly–
BRICE:	Daddy!
FATHER:	Ohhh! Why did you do that?
BRICE:	I wanna hit the ball.
FATHER:	Wait till we get off this first tee and I'll let you hit it. Now keep quiet–I'm gonna clout it! (SWISH .. CLICK)
BRICE:	Wheeeeeee!
FATHER:	Where'd it go, Snooks? I didn't see it.
BRICE:	It's right under your foot.
FATHER:	Uh–Guess I'm a little off my game! I've never played so badly before!
BRICE:	Have you ever played before, daddy?
FATHER:	(MIMICS HER) Yes, I've played before, daddy! Come on–let's walk down the fairway a little. These people watching make me nervous.
BRICE:	Ain't you gonna hit the ball, daddy?
FATHER:	Yes–as soon as we get a little closer to the hole. Come on–walk fast, Snooks.
BRICE:	Awight.

FATHER:	I'm going to drop the ball right here–I'll drop it over my shoulder so I won't be cheating. Now! This is about a four iron shot. Head down–eye on the ball–sway the hips–back slowly–
BRICE:	(ECHOES EVERY WORD SOFTLY)
FATHER:	Oh stop that! Just turn around for one second! That's it! Now! (SWISH... CLICK)
BRICE:	Did you hit it, daddy?
FATHER:	And how! Carried over sixty yards straight as an arrow–except it's a little out of bounds.
BRICE:	Is that good?
FATHER:	Not bad. Now come on–I don't want to lose that ball.
BRICE:	Let me hit it, daddy.
FATHER:	In a minute. I think the ball went out right about here.
BRICE:	Here's the ball, daddy. I found it.
FATHER:	Oh, what a bad lie! Why, nobody but a professional could make this shot to the green.
BRICE:	Let me do it, daddy.
FATHER:	All right, go ahead, you little smart aleck.
BRICE:	(LAUGHS)
FATHER:	I'll bet you won't even move the ball an inch. Take this club.
BRICE:	Which way shall I hit it?
FATHER:	Now you see that flag? Aim for that. Now just keep your head down–and your eye on the ball–don't tell me–

BRICE:	No, don't tell me. Don't tell me–I wanna hit it myself.
FATHER:	Well, go ahead.
BRICE:	Stand back. Stand back–(SWISH .... CLICK) .... (LAUGHS)
FATHER:	Well, I'll be–what a shot! Dead to the pin.
BRICE:	No good?
FATHER:	Why, it's a miracle! Come on–let's see how close it is.
BRICE:	Awight. (LAUGHS)
FATHER:	Why Snooks! Look at that ball–four inches from the cup!
BRICE:	What do I have to do now, daddy?
FATHER:	Make it go in that little hole!
BRICE:	Waaaaahhhhhhh!
FATHER:	Why what are you yelling about?
BRICE:	Why didn't you tell me when we was back there?
FATHER:	Ahhhhhh–come on! We're going home!
BRICE:	Waaaaaahhhhhhhh!
(MUSIC)	
(APPLAUSE)	

At the Hopital
(May 25, 1939)

MAXWELL HOUSE

5-25-39 (REVISED)

YOUNG: And now, Ladies and Gentlemen, here is Fanny Brice as Baby Snooks!

(MUSIC .... APPLAUSE)

YOUNG: Daddy, played by Hanley Stafford, has to visit his boss, who is sick in the hospital, to discuss some important business matters. Just to make things tough, Snooks has forced Daddy to take her with him. As the scene opens they are seated in the hospital waiting room. Listen....

BRICE: Is this the hospital, daddy?

FATHER: Yes, this is the hospital and be quiet, Snooks.

BRICE: It smells funny.

FATHER: Oh all hospitals smell like this.

BRICE: Why?

FATHER: On account of the antiseptic.

BRICE: Auntie who?

FATHER: Antiseptic. Antiseptic has a disagreeable odor.

BRICE: Why don't they give her a bath?

FATHER: No, listen, I'm not going to sit here and answer a lot of your nonsensical questions. And stop jumping up and down like a nervous cat!

BRICE: That man's doin' it. Look at him, daddy!

FATHER: Yes, he's an expectant father.

BRICE: Does he expect his father, daddy?

FATHER: No! He expects a baby!

BRICE: Why?

FATHER: Oh leave me alone. Snooks–stop pacing behind that poor fellow!

BRICE: Where's he goin' now, daddy?

FATHER: He's going in to speak to the doctor. He's nervous.

BRICE: Why?

FATHER: Maybe he knows what's coming! Come over here and sit next to me!

BRICE: Let me see your boss, daddy.

FATHER: We can't go in yet.

BRICE: Why?

FATHER: Because the nurse is in his room attending to him.

BRICE: What's the nurse doin', daddy?

FATHER: I don't know! I suppose she's doing what all nurses have to do!

BRICE:	(LAUGHS) My nursie used to have to take me no–
FATHER:	Now never mind that! It's a different kind of nurse–This is a trained nurse!
BRICE:	Ohhhh! She's doin' tricks in there?
FATHER:	No! Stop asking questions!
BRICE:	Why?
FATHER:	Oh just stop it–that's all! I don't want to be squabbling with you when we go in to see my boss. He's a very sick man.
BRICE:	What's the matter with him, daddy?
FATHER:	Well he's suffering from a respiratory condition.
BRICE:	(TRIES TO SAY IT) Respiratory condition?
FATHER:	Yes. When he gets out of here he's going to Switzerland for his lungs.
BRICE:	Did he leave them there?
FATHER:	No–he didn't leave them there! He's got them here!
BRICE:	Where?
	[Missing page]
BRICE:	Waaaaahhhhhh!
FATHER:	Well what are you yelling about?
BRICE:	'Cause you won't tell me his name!
FATHER:	Oh listen, Snooks–everybody has a first name and a last name. My boss has a first name and I have a first name. Do you know my first name?

BRICE:	Uh-huh.
FATHER:	Are you sure?
BRICE:	Uh-huh.
FATHER:	Well, what is it?
BRICE:	I dunno.
FATHER:	You do too! What does mummy call me?
BRICE:	Fathead.
FATHER:	She does not and don't remind me of it! Uh–(What kind of a child can you expect when you marry a fishwife!)
BRICE:	Huh?
FATHER:	Nothing! I just want to be sure you don't upset my boss the way you do me! In fact, I think we'd better have a little rehearsal before we go in there.
BRICE:	Awight, Daddy.
FATHER:	Now, I'll be the boss. Now don't forget–I'm very sick.
BRICE:	What's the matter with you, daddy?
FATHER:	Oh nothing's the matter with me!
BRICE:	You said you was sick.
FATHER:	I'm not sick–my boss is sick! And right now I'm my boss so I must be sick.
BRICE:	Awight–get sick, daddy.
FATHER:	Now don't worry–it's no job with you around. Now, let's try it. Here we go.

BRICE:	Where we goin'?
FATHER:	Oh nowhere! All right–come into the room. Be very quiet. Now, I'm sick in bed, there's nurses and doctors all around–and what's the first thing you say?
BRICE:	Show me the baby!
FATHER:	There isn't any baby!
BRICE:	When mummy got sick–
FATHER:	Oh that has nothing to do with this! You just say "I'm awful sorry you're sick, Mr. Watt. Here's some fruit." You understand?
BRICE:	Uh-huh.
FATHER:	Well let's try it again. All right–I'm sick. (GROANS) Ohhh!
BRICE:	Hello, Mr. Watt. I'm awful sorry you're sick–
FATHER:	That's good. Go on–where's the fruit?
BRICE:	I ate it on the way to the hospital.
FATHER:	What! Oh Snooks–did you really eat all that fruit?
BRICE:	I was hungry.
FATHER:	Ohhh! This is a fine how-do-you-do!
BRICE:	I'm fine, how do you do?
FATHER:	Oh stop that! I'm going to take you right home before you cause me any more trouble!
BRICE:	I wanna see the boss's lungs.

FATHER:	I told you, you can't see his lungs! Oh come on–let's get out of here!
BRICE:	I'll be good, daddy.
FATHER:	Well all right. Now just remember when you get in his room don't speak unless you're spoken to. If my boss tells you he's very sick you just say I'm awful sorry.
BRICE:	I'm awful sorry.
FATHER:	And to cheer him up when he says he doesn't think he'll recover you just say, "I hope they'll pull you thru".
BRICE:	I hope they'll pull you thru.
FATHER:	That's all you have to remember. I'm awful sorry–and I hope they'll pull you thru. Is that clear?
BRICE:	Uh-huh.
FATHER:	Oh there's the nurse signaling us. Now come on–we can go in … be quiet, Snooks.
	(DOOR CLOSES)
FATHER:	Well, hello, Mr. Watt.
BOSS:	(WEAKLY) Hello, Higgins.
FATHER:	(FORCED GAIETY) I–I've bought my little daughter to cheer you up.
BOSS:	Oh, hello, Snooks. It's nice of you to come.
BRICE:	How do you feel, Mr. Watt?
BOSS:	Well, Snooks–I think I'll recover.
BRICE:	Oh–I'm awful sorry.

BOSS:	Huh?
FATHER:	Ohhhh?
BOSS:	Hmmm. That's a nice thing to say to a man who's at death's door!
BRICE:	I hope they pull you thru.
FATHER:	Oh, Snooks!
BOSS:	Oh, so you brought her to cheer me up, eh, Higgins?
FATHER:	I–she doesn't know what she's saying Mr. Watt. I–
BRICE:	I wanna see your lungs.
BOSS:	Take that child out of here right away! Call the nurse!
BRICE:	(LAUGHS) His face is getting red, daddy.
FATHER:	You stop that! Sit there and don't open your mouth!
BOSS:	(GASPING) Ohhh! My pressure's going up. Higgins– I'm a sick man. Why do you do this to me?
FATHER:	Honestly, Mr. Watt, I didn't–
BOSS:	Do you realize what I've got? Did you ever hear of a disease that sends your blood pressure up sixty points in two seconds–makes your head spin and doesn't let you get a minute's rest!
FATHER:	Hear of it? Brother–I'm its father!
BRICE:	I wanna go home!
FATHER:	I told you to keep quiet! Mr. Watt–I'll come back later alone and we can go over the stuff then if you feel all right.

BOSS:	All right, Higgins. But I, I don't think I'll be able to sit up in bed.
FATHER:	Oh, no?
BOSS:	No, I–I'm a little stiff.
BRICE:	(LAUGHS)
BOSS:	What's so funny about that?
BRICE:	Daddy said you was a big stiff!
FATHER:	Ohhh! Come on–let's get out of here! (DOOR CLOSES) You wait, I'll–hey come here–don't run down that hall! They're feeding the babies.
BRICE:	I wanna hear the babies cry!
FATHER:	Oh, you do, do you? All right! (SLAP) There!
BRICE:	Waaaaahhhhhhh!
	(MUSIC ……. APPLAUSE)

PART TWO

OLSEN:	And now, ladies and gentlemen, Fannie Brice offers you her own version of one of the most haunting love stories in the world–the story of that lovelorn oriental maiden, Ming Ming Toy, which in our language means "poor little butterfly".
	(CHINESE MUSIC WITH CYMBALS FADES INTO BRICE SINGING WITH DIALECT)
BRICE:	(HUMS)

> Poor Butterfly
>
> Neath the blossoms waiting
>
> Poor Butterfly
>
> With a hot-cha-cha!

FATHER: Ming Ming Toy, my little daughter of the seven dragons, what are you singing?

BRICE: Ming Ming Toy sing song what Melican man is teaching her. I'm crazy for him!

FATHER: Remember, daughter, your love for this man will invoke the wrath of the Gods. (FOUR CHINESE GONGS) Do you hear the celestial gong? It is a warning. It struck four times. Gong! Gong! Gong! Gong! Do you know what that is?

BRICE: Sure–who don't know? That's Bert Lahr. Gong! Gong! Gong! Gong! ...Hark, what's that? (HORSE'S HOOFBEATS) Ah, I hear mine lover's footsteps!

FATHER: I have warned you. The rest is up to the Eleven Guardians of the Celestial Spirit.

BRICE: You mean twelve guardians, father.

FATHER: Eleven!

BRICE: No, twelve! Since the N.R.A. they took on another man!

FATHER: Farewell. (DOOR SLAM)

(KNOCK ON THE DOOR)

BRICE: Ha! It's mine Amelican sweetie–Captain Sam Singlefoot of the U.S. Haitch!

SAM:	Ship ahoy! Ahoy! Ming Toy! Ahoy!
BRICE:	What are you hollering oi-oi-oi–something hurts you?
SAM:	No, I'm talking sailor-talk. Shiver mine timbers! Come on, baby, give me a kiss!
BRICE:	Oh no–mine papa warned me. Me no kissee you Melican sailors.
SAM:	What's the matter–I'm a bad sailor?
BRICE:	Yeah–mine father said you're a wolf in ship's clothing.
SAM:	Listen, I'm a different kind of sailor. I don't drink–I don't smoke–and I don't swear.
BRICE:	Is that so! Do you make your own dresses too?
SAM:	Stop cracking wise, little butterfly! To come to you I traveled all the way up the Yangtze River!
BRICE:	You did! Did you pass the Yangtze Stadium?
SAM:	Come on, Cherry Blossom, we'll sit under that big apple tree.
BRICE:	No, no, me no comee!
SAM:	Why, you don't trust me or you don't trust yourself?
BRICE:	I trust you and I trust me, but I don't trust the two of us together.
SAM:	Ti-ti-ti! The two of us together! Look at that wonderful apple tree! I bet you it's been going on plenty romantical things under this tree. If that apple tree could talk what would he say?
BRICE:	He would say "pipe down, sailor, I'm a banana tree."

SAM:	Listen, Butterfly, if we're gonna get married, I would at least like to get one sample of your kissing.
BRICE:	Oh, no. Me no give you samples. But me give you references.
SAM:	Ah-ha! References! Didn't I send you a telegram saying you shouldn't let nobody kiss you?
BRICE:	I know–but it came five minutes too late.
SAM:	Mine Butterfly, you're gorgeous! I can't wait no longer! If I kiss you, will you call your father?
BRICE:	Why, you want to kissee the whole family?
SAM:	No, no. I'm crazy only for you. Look, I brought you this beautiful fan for a present. Every time you fan yourself you should think of me! Now will you love me forever?
BRICE:	I don't know, but I'll love you for the present!
SAM:	Come–sit with me in the garden. Wait! Why do you put the fan on the chair before you sit down?
BRICE:	It's a Chinee custom. Evlybody likee to sit on fannee!
SAM:	Ming Toy–I got to ask you something very confidential. Will you go away with me to America?
BRICE:	Captain Sam, that will bring shame on the house of mine ancestors. They was the biggest peoples from our tribe. Mine grandfather, One Bum Hip, was a big man. Mine great-grandfather One Bum Knee, was a bigger man. But mine great-great-grandfather–One Bum–he was the biggest bum of them all!
SAM:	Well, since I couldn't marry you, couldn't you give me something to remember you by?

BRICE:	Yes, Ming Toy give you her ivory comb. Here–put it in your hip pocket and keep it close to your heart.
SAM:	Thank you, my little star of the morning. Here's a memento for you. It's mine old watch. It don't tick no more, but you can have it.
BRICE:	Uh-uh. No tickee, no watchee. (FOGHORN BLOWS)
SAM:	That's the signal from mine ship, little Butterfly. I got to leave you. I'm sailing away and never coming back.
BRICE:	Allee lightee Sam. Me no say a word if you go. Me no cly. Go ahead.
SAM:	O.K.–I'm going.
BRICE:	(YELLS) Sam! Don't leave me! Take me with you!
SAM:	(WITH DEEP EMOTION) Mine poor butterfly. I couldn't do this because your kind and mine kind couldn't be happy together.
BRICE:	(SOBBING) What's the matter, Sam? Ain't we brothers under the skin?–I mean, sisters?
SAM:	Darling–I would like to give you one kiss before I'm going.
BRICE:	(SNIFFLES) All right, Sam.

SAM:	(SMACK)
	Mm-hah! Let me kiss you again!
BRICE:	(SNIFFLES)
	Who stops you?
SAM:	(SMACK)
	Mm-ha! That's fine! Wait, little butterfly, where are you going?
BRICE:	That kissing reminds me–I got to put onions in the chop suey.
SAM:	Don't leave me even for a second! (FOGHORN) You hear? The time is short! Let me hold you in mine arms.
BRICE:	(SNIFFLES)
	Allee lightee! Tell me, Captain Sam, are you Santa Claus?
SAM:	No, why?
BRICE:	Then leave mine stocking alone.
SAM:	Ti-ti-ti! Santa Claus! Why don't you call me a real pet name?
BRICE:	Allee lightee! I'll call you opium.
SAM:	Opium? That's a dope!
BRICE:	That's right!
SAM:	Well, I got to get back to the ship. (FOGHORN) Mine goodness! That's the last call for supper! Goodbye, mine little butterfly.

BRICE: (SOBS)

Goodbye, Sam.

SAM: (ALSO SOBS)

Do you love me?

BRICE: Oh, Sam, I–(SMACK) love (SMACK) you (SMACK) so (SMACK) much (SMACK) I (SMACK) don't know how I could live (SMACK) without mine great big Melican man (SMACK).

SAM: Goodbye, mine butterfly!

BRICE: Goodbye!

(FOGHORN)

SAM: Kiss me again!

BRICE: I can't!

SAM: What's the matter? Don't you love me anymore?

BRICE: Sure I do, but I got to take a rest?

SAM: (CRYING THRU ENTIRE SCENE)

Well, goodbye.

BRICE: (CRYING THRU ENTIRE SCENE)

Goodbye!

SAM: Don't look at any other sailors.

BRICE: I will!

SAM: Write me every day.

BRICE: I won't!

SAM: Don't forget.

BRICE:	I will!
SAM:	Goodbye, Butterfly.
BRICE:	I won't… I mean goodbye!
	(FOGHORN)
SAM:	(SOBS)
	Goodbye, Butterfly!
BRICE:	(SOBS BITTERLY)
	Goodbye, Sam!
	(DOOR SLAM)
BRICE:	Sam! Sam!
SAM:	What is it?
BRICE:	You forgot something!
SAM:	What?
BRICE:	You forgot to say goodbye!

Elopement
(story treatment)

Daddy is in a hurry to get to his office, but is delayed by the disappearance of his razor - he's all set to go to a barber for a shave, when it dawns on him that perhaps Snooks knows the razor's whereabouts... He calls to her and she appears with her puss all smeared up with what Daddy mistakes for strawberry jam, but on closer inspection he finds it to be lipstick.

"Where's my razor?" he hollers, and Snooks explains that she loaned it to his future son-in-law... She goes on to tell him that she and Herby Jones, feeling that they're getting on in years, have decided to get married - and this is the day they're eloping.

She has loaned the razor to eight year old Herby, she tells Daddy, in order that he might be clean shaven for the marriage ceremony. When Daddy tells her that a boy his age couldn't possibly have a beard, she explains that they overcame this by shaving off his eyebrows.

Daddy doesn't see the humor of the situation until she asks him to be Best Man - then he decides to show her the seriousness of marriage and begins to explain the pitfalls. When she asks him why he got married, he can't answer... She still isn't convinced when Daddy gets through explaining, she tells him that she must be on her way because Herby is outside waiting with the elopement Scooter.

Daddy decides to stall her a bit by asking where they're going on their honeymoon - she tells him Niagara Falls. He then wants to know if she'll have enough clothes for so long a journey, so she trots out her packed valise in order to convince him. Upon being opened, it's found to contain, among other things, two dolls, a ball and jacks, a box of Daddy's cigars, and eight bars of peanut brittle.

Daddy asks her how long she intends to be gone, and when she tells him thirty or forty years he's almost tempted to let her go. He restrains himself, tho, and seeks to further convince Snooks by showing her that she's still a little too young to be married... he brings out the family album, and shows her pictures of himself and his wife at the time of their marriage. Uncle Louie is in one picture and Daddy explains that he was the Best Man at the wedding. Snooks wants to know if Uncle Louie was the best man, why didn't Mommy marry him? Daddy can't understand it, either.

He goes looking for the old love letters he and his wife had sent each other in their youth, but Snooks saves him the trouble by explaining that she borrowed them. It seems that she had wanted to write Herby a love letter and she thought she'd save time by sending him one of her Mommy's.

The phone rings and it's Herby's Pop. Daddy answers it and is a little upset when Mr. Jones addresses him as "Baby Dumplings" - he had evidently been reading the love letters.

The two men get into a heated argument over the worth of their respective children and each declares that they wouldn't let the kids marry if they lived to be a hundred. They both hang up sore - there is a pause, until Snooks asks Daddy, "Is it all right to get married now?" "No!" he bellows - and when she cries, he tells her that she can get married later in the summer. She replies that it's too late by then. Daddy a little bit shocked, wants to know why. And she tells him that School vacation will be in effect, and there's no sense in getting married on your vacation.

They both laugh - Daddy kisses her - Snooks agrees to forget about marriage for a while. She brings a delighted Daddy back his razor, and he hums as he prepares to shave - however, he soon discovers that she's done away with all his blades - so he departs for his office leaving Snooks spanked and himself unshaven.

Painting
(full script of Good News 1939, September 29, 1938)

MAXWELL HOUSE

presents

"GOOD NEWS OF 1939"

September 29, 1938

#40

(REVISED)

CAST

1. Ted Pearson
2. George Jessel
3. Spencer Tracy
4. Rita Johnson
5. Francis Wallace
6. Frank Morgan
7. Fanny Brice
8. Phil Regan
9. Christine Wells
10. Hanley Stafford
11. Meredith Willson and Orchestra
12. Max Terr Chorus

MAXWELL HOUSE
Routine

SEPTEMBER 29, 1938
(Revised)

Page		
	OPENING	
	MORGAN – JESSEL	
	1 – 1C	MORGAN – "SAM, THE COLLEGE LEADER MAN"
	2 – 2F	BABY SNOOKS – "DADDY'S MASTERPIECE"
	REGAN – "WITH YOU ON MY MIND"	
4 – 4C	"TOO HOT TO HANDLE" – DEVINNA-ROSSON-JESSEL	
5 – 5A	COMMERCIAL	
6	BAND – "THE YAM"	
7 – 7C	MORGAN – WILLSON – JESSEL – DEVINNA	
	STATION BREAK	
8A	WELLS – "ROSE MARIE" MEDLEY	
9 – 9H	DRAMA – "HE WHO GETS SLAPPED" – TRACY-JOHNSON	
10	BOND – "I'M GONNA LOCK MY HEART"	
11 – 11C	"IF MEN ATTENDED FASHION SHOWS AS WOMEN DO"	
	Tracy-Jessel-Morgan-Willson	

12 – 12A	COMMERCIAL
	CONCERT HALL – "SLEEPING BEAUTY"
14 – 14B	FRANCIS WALLAGE – JESSEL
	CLOSING

PEARSON: Maxwell House Coffee presents ... Good News of 1939!

(MUSIC: IN AND FADE)

PEARSON: The makers of Maxwell House Coffee welcome you to another hour of fine entertainment from the Metro-Goldwyn-Mayer Studios in Hollywood with our regular cast of favorites, plus Francis Wallace, nationally known football authority, and the guest star you're all waiting to hear – Spencer Tracy. And your host for the evening, George Jessel!

(MUSIC OUT)

(APPLAUSE)

JESSEL: Thank you Ted Pearson. Good evening, ladies and gentlemen. I feel very honored this evening that I have been called upon to appear as your surprise master of ceremonies. My pals, Robert Young and Robert Taylor are both a couple of pretty busy fellows - Bob Taylor with a new picture for Mervyn LeRoy called "Stand Up And Fight", and Bob Yong doing some final scenes in Joan Crawford's new picture, "The Shining Hour". They've asked me to pinch-hit for them – so here I am. And why not. After all, what have they got that makes me photograph like a moose?

MORGAN:	All right, fellows! (POLICE WHISTLE)
CHORUS:	RAH! RAH! RAH! RAH!
	MOR-GAN FOR SENA-TAH!
JESSEL:	Hey – what's goin' on here?
CHORUS:	ALLA KAZAM KAZEE KAZOO
	HE'S THE MAN FOR ME AND YOU.
JESSEL:	What is this?
CHORUS:	RAH RAH RAH RAH
	RAH RAH RAH RAH
	RAH RAH RAH RAH
	RAH
	(BAND INTO BOOLA BOOLA)
MORGAN:	(SINGS)
	Boola boola
	How do you doola
	Don't be a foola
	Vote for me –
JESSEL:	(OVER MUSIC) Wait a minute!
MORGAN:	(SINGS)
	Boola boola
	Make a roola
	Keepa coola

	Vote for me!
	(CHEERS, WHISTLES, ETC.)
JESSEL:	That's a nice entrance, Morgan. What time does the balloon go up?
MORGAN:	Why Georgie! My old friend Jessel! How are you?
JESSEL:	Fine, senator. How's Madame Senator and all the little representatives?
MORGAN:	I wouldn't know, Georgie. I haven't been home for four days, they tell me. I've been busy doing a little political taxidermy.
JESSEL:	Political taxidermy! What's that?
MORGAN;	Stuffing ballot boxes. (GIGGLES)
JESSEL:	That's what I like about you, Frank. You're a thief after my own heart.
MORGAN:	What's the difference – a few votes more or less – I'm bound to be elected by a huge majority anyhow – on account of my record.
JESSEL:	Your record? Then you burned it.
MORGAN:	Yes. WHAT? Oh I'm not speaking of my public record, Georgie, I'm talking about my private life. The voters want a man they can trust, and I'm known all over the country as a model citizen, a man of regular habits.
JESSEL:	Frank, don't make those fantastic claims! Regular habits – it's only three nights ago you were arrested for whistling at a strange woman on Hollywood Boulevard.
MORGAN:	Er – yes. Well, that's one of my regular habits.

JESSEL: You know Frank, you ought to let me manage your campaign and I'd keep you out of trouble. I handled a campaign for a man back East, and in two days I got him forty thousand votes.

MORGAN: Honestly?

JESSEL: What's the difference – I got 'em. But all's fair in love and politics. The main thing is to know where to find the votes.

MORGAN: Oh, don't worry about me finding votes. I spent the whole day today canvassing the colleges. This afternoon I went to a football game and got fifteen thousand votes right there.

JESSEL: Did you go after the co-eds?

MORGAN: Did I? (GIGGLES) Till that stadium policeman saw me --- OH! You mean their votes. I appealed to all the voters regardless of sex or political affiliation. There was only one unfortunate incident the whole afternoon.

JESSEL: What was that, Senator?

MORGAN: The half-back on the visiting team was getting off a big punt and he kicked me.

JESSEL: That's terrible – where'd he kick you?

MORGAN: Right on the fifty-yard line! Why, I could barely limp over to the bandstand.

JESSEL: Bandstand? What were you doing at the bandstand?

MORGAN: Didn't you ever hear of my career in college?

JESSEL: No.

MORGAN:	Hit it, fellows.
	"SAM THE COLLEGE LEADER MAN"
	MORGAN & ORCHESTRA
	(APPLAUSE)

BABY SNOOKS

JESSEL:	And now, ladies and gentleman, I'd advise you all to run for cover – but leave room for me. Here comes Fanny Brice as that nerve-tearing rascal – BABY SNOOKS!
	(MUSIC) (APPLUASE)
JESSEL:	Tonight, Daddy, played by Hanley Stafford, is happily engaged in his private little hobby – painting. Although his wife is not of the same opinion, Daddy fancies himself as an artist. We find him laboring in the cellar on his great masterpiece hoping he will not be disturbed. But Fate is indeed unkind – Listen.
	(SOUND OF FOOTSTEPS)
FATHER:	Who is it?
BRICE:	Hello, daddy.
FATHER:	Oh, it's you!
BRICE:	Why are you wearing mummy's dress?
FATHER:	It's not mummy's dress – it's a smock!
BRICE:	It looks like mummy's dress!
FATHER:	Well, it's not! All artists wear these! Now leave me alone!

BRICE:	I wanna watch you paint.
FATHER:	Really? All right, darling – just sit quietly and don't make a sound.
BRICE:	Awight ….. Daddy?
FATHER:	Yes?
BRICE:	Why you painting in the cellar?
FATHER:	Because I like to paint down here – and please don't bother me with questions.
BRICE:	Last night you was painting in the kitchen.
FATHER:	I know – but I like to paint in the cellar better.
BRICE:	Why?
FATHER:	Because – because the light is better! Besides it gives me – more the feeling of the true artist – cramped quarters – dreary-looking – yes, it inspires me. Do you understand why I like to paint in the cellar?
BRICE:	Yes, daddy – mummy kicked you out of the kitchen!
FATHER:	Sure – what does she know about --- SNOOKS! You mind your own business! All great artists painted under difficulties. Why, even Rembrandt's greatest masterpiece was painted on an empty stomach.
BRICE:	Who's stomach, daddy?
FATHER:	Rembrandt's!
BRICE:	Didn't it come off when he took a bath?
FATHER:	Oh, what's the use – keep quiet!
BRICE:	Daddy?

FATHER:	What?
BRICE:	You got some paint on mummy's dress!
FATHER:	I told you it's not mummy's dress! Go on upstairs!
BRICE:	I don't wanna!
FATHER:	Snooks – don't touch my canvas!
BRICE:	What is it, daddy?
FATHER:	(DEFIANTLY) It's a sea picture – and it's great, too, no matter what anybody says! (HOPEFULLY) How do you like it, Snooks?
BRICE:	Oooooooh – I like it.
FATHER:	(TRIUMPHANTLY) There you are! A child judges art instinctively. Of course she likes it.
BRICE:	Are you gonna sell it, daddy?
FATHER:	Oh, no. I only painted it for my own amusement.
BRICE:	(LAUGHS)
FATHER:	What's the matter?
BRICE:	I think it's funny, too!
FATHER:	What's funny about it – this is a wonderful study! I'm going to call it "Faith".
BRICE:	Why?
FATHER:	Well, you see that little boat being tossed about by those high waves? And do you notice that sailor on board with his hands raided to heaven? He has faith that he'll be rescued.

BRICE: What's faith, daddy?

FATHER: Well, you can see the boat and you can see the sailor – but if I told you there was a pork chop on that boat and you believed me, that would be faith, understand?

BRICE: Uh-huh.

FATHER: All right – what is faith?

BRICE: A pork chop on a boat!

FATHER: Oh, go away and let me finish this painting.

BRICE: I don't wanna.

FATHER: Then sit in the corner and play.

BRICE: What shall I do, daddy?

FATHER: DO NOTHING!

BRICE: How will I know when I'm finished?

FATHER: Oh, for heaven's sakes! Here – take this crayon and draw on a piece of paper.

BRICE: What shall I draw, daddy?

FATHER: Anything! Hmmmm – guess I'll have to highlight the side of this boat a little… gotta be very steady and careful – just a touch –

BRICE: Daddy!

FATHER: Snooks! Don't yell like that!

BRICE: Why?

FATHER: You made me smudge my painting! What do you want?

BRICE:	How many kinds of milk is there?
FATHER:	Oh, I don't know – five or six, I guess. There's buttermilk – whole milk – skim milk ---- or ---
BRICE:	Milk of magnesia?
FATHER:	Ye—NO! Why do you want to know how many kinds of milk there are?
BRICE:	I'm drawing a picture of a cow –
FATHER:	Well?
BRICE:	I wanna know how many faucets of put on it!
FATHER:	Oh, stop that nonsense! Draw something else.
BRICE:	Awight … (SINGS TO HERSELF)
FATHER:	Don't sing – just draw.
BRICE:	Why?
FATHER:	Because you make me nervous and my hand shakes. Now, keep quiet while I darken this wave… Easy, now ---
BRICE:	(YELLS) Daddy!
FATHER:	Ohhh! You made me spoil it again. What is it?
BRICE:	I drawed a picture.
FATHER:	Picture! That horrible mess! What is it supposed to be?
BRICE:	Uncle Louie!
FATHER:	Snooks, you know as well as I do that doesn't look very much like Uncle Louie.
BRICE:	Don't it?

FATHER:	No!
BRICE:	Then I'll put a tail on it and call it a monkey!
FATHER:	Snooks – go upstairs and let me work! And stop fooling with those paints! Snooks – put down that brush!
BRICE:	I wanna paint with it, daddy.
FATHER:	No – it's very expensive. That's a camel's hair brush.
BRICE:	Huh?
FATHER:	It's a camel's hair brush.
BRICE:	How does he do it?
FATHER:	How does who do what?
BRICE:	How does the camel brush his hair with it?
FATHER:	The camel doesn't brush his hair! The hair in this brush is supposed to come from a camel, but it's really made out of hog bristles which don't come from a pig but are taken from a beaver and that's why they call it camel's hair!
BRICE:	Do you feel all right, daddy?
FATHER:	I feel fine! (PLEADING) Go away and let me enjoy myself – please.
BRICE:	Are you having fun, daddy?
FATHER:	(ALMOST CRYING) Yes – it's the only pleasure I get in this house – leave me alone! I'm very happy down here!
BRICE:	I'll be good if you show me some more pictures.
FATHER:	(EAGERLY) Would you really like to see them?
BRICE:	Uh-huh.

FATHER:	Well, I'm going to show you one that I've never shown anybody. If you like it, Snooks – it'll make me very happy .... Here – this is my masterpiece.
BRICE:	Oooooooh – I like it.
FATHER:	You do? Does it look real?
BRICE:	Uh-huh – it's so real it makes me hungry.
FATHER:	Hungry? Why should this painting make you hungry? It's supposed to be a beautiful sunset.
BRICE:	Ohhhh ... I thought it was a fried egg!
FATHER:	WHAT! What do you know about art? Go on upstairs – quick, before I get mad!
BRICE:	I don't wanna.
FATHER:	(YELLS) Get out of here!
BRICE:	If you don't let me stay here I'll eat the paints!
FATHER:	Don't – that's poison! SNOOKS! Come here!
BRICE:	I won't.
FATHER:	Look out for that easel! SNOOKS!
	(CRASH ... SOUND OF CANVAS TEARING)
FATHER:	(GROANS) Ohhh – my beautiful painting – ruined – smeared all over with paint – the canvas is torn – Ohhhhhhh!
BRICE:	I think I'll go upstairs now.
FATHER:	Wait a minute! I want to give you something!
BRICE:	What?

FATHER:	This! --- (SLAP)
BRICE:	WAAAHHHHHHHHH!!
	(MUSIC UP)
	(APPLAUSE)
JESSEL:	Here's a young fellow whose singing always gives me a thrill. Believe me, it's my pleasure to introduce Phil Regan, singing "With You On My Mind."
	WITH YOU ON MY MIND REGAN
	ORCHESTRA
	(APPLAUSE)
	DEVOMMA – ROSSON
JESSEL:	Last night, ladies and gentlemen, I had the pleasure of seeing the new Clark Gable – Myrna Loy picture, "Too Hot To Handle", which the critics predict will be one of the biggest hits of the movie season. It's a picture full of thrills and some of the most sensational photography of a primitive country that I've ever seen – shots made in the Netherlands Guiana – about 174 miles from the famous French penal colony at Devil's Island. The men responsible for this part of the picture are with us tonight, -- Clyde DeVinna, cameraman – and Dick Rosson, director. (APPLAUSE) Dick – Clyde – I understand you were down in Netherlands Guiana for about six weeks.
DEVINNA:	That's right, George.

JESSEL: Clyde, I've always had an ambition to appear in a theatre down there. Why, I can just close my eyes and see my name in lights – George Jessel – at Loew's Netherlands Guiana!

DEVINNA: I wish you'd been there last summer…although we didn't have much time to go to shows.

JESSEL: You were on a rush assignment, weren't you, Clyde?

DEVINNA: Well, just to give you an idea – when we were starting down there, we saw posters of "Too Hot To Handle" in Miami, Florida. We really hustled, George. We airmailed all our film as soon as it was shot.

JESSEL: Of course, you had a script with you, I suppose. Is that right, Dick?

ROSSON: Yes. The script called for certain things that weren't exactly a cinch to do. Tell George about our long shot of the native village, Clyde.

DEVINNA: Well, we were taking shots of a little native village right in the middle of the thickest jungle I ever saw, and –

JESSEL: Just let me interrupt a second, Clyde. Ladies and gentlemen, Mr. Clyde DeVinna is one cameraman that's a connoisseur of jungles. He spent two years in Africa filming "Trader Horn" and also photographed "White Shadows in the South Seas". He never got lost in a jungle, but it took him two hours to find an exit from the Coliseum after the football game last Saturday.

DEVINNA: Anyway, George, we were photographing this native village, and we received an order from Hollywood for a long shot of it. Well, you know that all you do in a long shot is get a long ways from your subject, aim the camera

	at it, and crank her. But the trouble with this long shot was that the jungle was tight around the village, and you couldn't haul your camera back into the woods and shoot, because the jungle was so thick.
JESSEL:	Couldn't you get up on a hill and shoot down?
DEVINNA:	Could have, except for one thing.
JESSEL:	What was that?
DEVINNA:	No hill. Whole country was as flat as a pool table, George.
JESSEL:	Like my singing.
ROSSON:	As a matter of fact it was a physical impossibility to get a long shot of the village.
JESSEL:	I see. So what did you do, boys?
DEVINNA:	We found a tree about a hundred and twenty-five feet high, spent two days cutting away branches that shut off the view, rigged a block and tackle and hoisted the 300-pound camera a hundred feet up the tree, then I climbed up and cranked out a long shot.
JESSEL:	I remember the shot in the picture. Tell me Dick Rosson, did you have any other tough assignments?
ROSSON:	Yes, we were supposed to photograph an actor carrying another fellow in his arms, and wading into the river till he reached an airplane, then putting him aboard. We lined up the shot down by the bank of the river, with a lot of natives standing around watching and our man was just about to step into the river when one of the chiefs rushed into the scene and commanded us to stop.

JESSEL: A mere native chief gives orders to a director? They can't do that!

DEVINNA: In Netherland Guiana, they can.

ROSSON: Well, George, the chief sent up to the village and had somebody bring down a lot of fresh killed beef – and just dipped it into the stream. When he took it out there was no more meat on it – stripped clean as a whistle.

JESSEL: Sharks?

ROSSON: No – they were Piranhas, a little cannibal fish. Their teeth are so sharp, they can take a bite out of your leg without your even feeling it.

JESSEL: I know – like Eddie Cantor. Well I remember that shot in the picture, too, and I think you wound up taking the chap to the plane in a canoe, is that right?

DEVINNA: That's right. The fish don't eat canoes.

JESSEL: If they did, that would really be news. Well, boys, it's a great picture. No wonder – when you have a fine producer like Larry Weingarten you're bound to get great entertainment. And with a director like Jack Conway and stars like Clark Gable and Myrna Loy with Walter Cannolly, Walter Pidgeon and Leo Carrillo. The picture is a thrill a minute all the way, and the contribution you fellows made will never be forgotten. Thank you Dick Rosson and Clyde DeVinna.

(APPLAUSE)

(FIRST HALF OF SHOW)

JESSEL:	And now, Ted Pearson.
PEARSON:	Thanks. Friends … let me ask you … how long has it been since you've sat back in your chair after breakfast, or after dinner, and exclaimed –
1ST MAN:	Say! That was one grand cup of coffee.
PEARSON:	My guess is that because thousands more are drinking Maxwell House these days, why naturally more people are saying just that about their cup of coffee. Here's the reason. Everybody who is drinking Maxwell House today is enjoying coffee that's even richer and more delicious than ever before. So, let me ask you – have you tried Maxwell House lately? If you haven't, then we believe you're missing the greatest coffee pleasure in your life. You see, Maxwell House Coffee has actually been improved in two important ways. First …
2ND MAN:	This already superb blend of the world's choice coffees has been still further enriched. You'll taste this extra richness with your very first cup. You'll notice a new smoothness and mellowness that'll satisfy you, we believe, beyond any coffee you've ever known.
PEARSON:	And second….
2ND MAN:	This wonderfully enriched Maxwell House blend is now roasted by a new process called radiant roast. Now, radiant heat penetrates each coffee bean… gives it not just a surface roasting…but roasts it evenly….through and through. Naturally, this means still more full flavor in your cup of coffee.

(FIRST HALF OF SHOW – 2)

PEARSON: And that extra flavor, friends, is what you're missing if you haven't tried Maxwell House Coffee lately. Discover this better coffee. It's at your grocers now ... in the same familiar blue super-vacuum can you've always known. Tomorrow enjoy this coffee that ... now more than ever ... is good to the last drop.

(MUSIC BRIDGE)

JESSEL: Here's Meredith Willson and his orchestra giving you their interpretation of the newest dance craze created by Irving Berlin for the Astaire-Rogers musical "Carefree"... THE YAM!!

All right, Willson...make it a "YAM" session!!

"THE YAM" ORCHESTRA

(APPLAUSE)

MORGAN – WILLSON – JESSEL – DeVINNA (REVISED)

MERE: Say, Mr. Jessel –

JESSEL: Yes, Meredith?

MERE: Er – Clyde DeVinna wants you to introduce him to Frank Morgan.

JESSEL: On the level? Clyde, do you mean that?

DeV: Yes, I've been wanting to meet him the worst way.

JESSEL: Any way you meet Morgan – that's the worst way. But if you want it, all right. Hey, Frank! Frank!

MORG:	(ENTERING) Well, that's the last time I play cards with those musicians. Those fellows cheat.
MERE:	Now wait a minute, Frank, don't accuse my men of sharp practice.
JESSEL:	No – Willson's men don't practice at all.
MORG:	Well, all I know is I sat there with three aces full, and that thieving piccolo player comes up with a straight flush, ace high.
JEESSEL:	So the guy had a straight flush! What makes you think he's cheating?
MORG:	Well, I know what I dealt him. What a crook!
JESS:	Frank, take those kings out of your sleeve and shake hands with Clyde DeVinna.
MORG:	Oh yes, I know your brother, Andy DeVinna.
DeV:	Devine.
MORG:	I think it's ducky, too. He's a nice kid.
DeV:	No relation, Mr. Morgan.
JESSEL:	Frank, this man is Clyde DeVinna. He fools with cameras, and he's also a registered voter.
MORG:	Oh! Cameras, huh?
JESSEL:	(TO AUDIENCE) That'll give him four minutes of fast lies.
MORG:	Mr. DeVinna, I am profoundly interested in anybody that loves photography. Especially the vast army of fellows like yourself—the dubs.

JESSEL:	Dubs. You're an expert, eh, Morgan?
MORG:	Fellows, years ago, I was known as Brownie Morgan, the snapshot king. That was before I invented the oscillating lens, the double reversible shutter, the one-way inverted finder, and the standing-sitting-running dive.
DeV:	Are you really familiar with the camera, Mr. Morgan?
MORG:	Am I? Who do you think invented slow motion?
JESSEL:	Two Scotchmen reaching for a dinner check.
MORG:	A cheap quip, worthy of the variety stages.
JESSEL:	I wish I could get on one.
MORG:	Don't try to change the subject – I could talk for hours of my stage career. I'm talking to Mr. DeVinna now about photography. Tell me, sir, do you get your snaps developed at the drugstore?
DeV:	Well, I –
MORG:	Don't apologize, my friend. It's as good a place as any.
JESS:	Frank—Mr. DeVinna here has done quite a bit of work with the camera. His last assignment was "Too Hot to Handle".
MORG:	It was? They should have sent for me! Nothing's too hot for Morgan to handle. Why when I was a newsreel cameraman I spent four successive years covering the beauty contests in Atlantic City. I didn't get any pictures, but I did plenty of work in the dark room. (GIGGLES) Surprising what you can develop there!
DeV:	Mr. Morgan, I used to be a newsreel cameraman myself.

MORG:	You were! Then you must remember me! I made my reputation in 1924 covering the Coolidge inaugural address and the eruption of Mt. Vesuvius.
DeV:	Wait a minute, Mr. Morgan. Both those things happened on the same day, three thousand miles apart.
MORG:	They did?
DeV:	Yes! How could you be in both places at the same time?
MORG:	(MUMBLES) Both – places. Places, places, places. Errrrrrrrr---Yes, well, that year I was leading a double life! (GIGGLES) – (I know he'll believe that!)
DeV:	I still don't understand it, Mr. Morgan.
MORG:	Skepticism is every man's privilege. Nevertheless, I got both pictures.
DeV:	Well, all I can say is that a shot of the Vesuvius eruption, and of Mr. Coolidge's inaugural address, should be pretty valuable.
MORG:	They would have been worth a king's ransom, my friend, had I not made a careless oversight which resulted in a double exposure.
DeV:	Really? What happened?
MORG:	Well, we ran the film in the projection room, and as soon as Mr. Coolidge began to speak, molten lava ran out of his mouth, smoke poured out of his ears, and believe it or not, his coat tails were on fire. (This is going too far, fellows, I don't believe it myself!)
DeV:	Well, Mr. Morgan, I covered Lindbergh's take-off in 1928.

MORG: Is that so?

JESSEL: Excuse me, gentlemen – did you know that the average annual rainfall in New Jersey is thirteen and a half inches?

MORG: What's that got to do with photography?

JESSEL: Nothing – but I haven't said anything since page two. All right, fellows, you can get back into your camera work.

MORG: Jessel, for a man who knows nothing about photography, you're being very negative. What were you saying, DeVinna?

DeV: I meant to ask you, Mr. Morgan – have you had any experience with three dimensional photography?

MORG: Son, I solved all the problems of three dimensional photography and three dimensional projection in the year 1922. When I had it perfected I took a picture of a locomotive speeding along at sixty miles an hour and projected it before an audience at the Pismo Avenue Theatre in Long Beach, California.

DeV: What happened?

MORG: It was so real the locomotive ran right off the screen and killed fifty people! It'll never be popular.

DEVINNA: What was your first experience as a cameraman, Mr. Morgan?

MORGAN: My first experience, Clyde? I'll never forget it. It was the greatest triumph of native intelligence over stupidity, experience, and money that has ever been recorded in history's pages. I was a cub on the old New York Sphere

	at the time, and the city editor sent me down to get pictures of the arrival of Fulton's new invention, the steamboat, when it arrived in New York Harbor.
DEVINNA:	But Mr. Morgan, the steamboat was invented in 1845!
MORGAN:	That's right, but there were no cameras in those days. I went down to the harbor, a raw country boy, apples in my cheeks, stars in my eyes, and a pawn-ticket in my pocket.
JESSEL:	A pawn ticket!
MORGAN:	I'd had to pawn my grandfather's watch to get money for my camera.
DEVINNA:	You must have got a pretty good camera with all that money.
MORGAN:	Well – no. Even in those days you couldn't get much of a camera for 28 cents. What did my grandfather care about what time it was?
DEVINNA:	Twenty-eight cents!
MORGAN:	A small sum, no doubt. But my ingenuity was equal to the challenge. I found an old Maxwell House Coffee can, bored a hole in the end of it, bought a percolator top in the dime store for a lens, and constructed an ingenious shutter from a pair of old sugar tongs. I rushed to the pier and stood with the other photographers waiting for the historic event.
DEVINNA:	I suppose the other boys had pretty classy equipment, didn't they?

MORGAN:	Did they? Eight million dollars' worth of cameras were on the pier that day. Graflax, reflex, duplex, triplex, and Kleenex. I'll ever forget how they simpered at me when I arrived with my home-made coffee-can camera.
DEVINNA:	Did you really hope to get a picture?
MORGAN:	My confidence never flagged. But just as the pretty craft slid trimly into her slip, a cowardly representative of the Daily Bugle gave me a push from the rear (I can feel it to this day) and dumped me into the churning waters of the North River.
DEVINNA:	What a terrible break!
MORGAN:	Never fear! A Morgan turns misfortune into opportunity! There I was, six feet under water, as the Claremont passed above me – and what did I do? I focused carefully and made a daring underwater shot – the first angle shot in history! Having snapped the shutter, I rose to the surface, swam ashore with the camera between my teeth, and rushed home, still dripping, to develop my precious film. To save time I poured the solution right into the camera, let it stand for three minutes over an infra-red heating lamp, took off the lid of the coffee can, and what do you think?
DE VINNA:	You had the greatest picture of them all!
MORGAN:	No, but I had a darn fine cup of coffee! (GIGGLES) Don't forget to vote for me, Devinna! So long!
	(APPLAUSE)

STATION BREAK

PEARSON: Well, folks, I imagine you won't need more than one guess to tell what comes next in the order of the evening – right – that cheery custom of ours ... a moment of relaxation over a steaming, fragrant cup of the new Maxwell House. So, we're inviting all of you to join us now in a friendly cup of this coffee that buoys you up and never lets you down.

And of course, with the new Maxwell House, you'll find that cup of coffee more delicious than ever. You'll note an extra richness ... a smoothness and mellowness ... that'll satisfy you, we believe, beyond any coffee you've ever tasted.

All right, Meredith – if you'll pour out the music, we'll pour out the coffee.

(MUSIC UP AND FADE FOR STATION ANNOUNCEMENT)

PEARSON: We now pause briefly for station identification.

JESSEL: We continue the second half of this edition of Good News of 1939 in which you will hear Spencer Tracy and Rita Johnson in the dramatic classic, "He Who Gets Slapped"... Francis Wallace giving you flashes on the football outlook for Saturday, and another one of those hilarious satires – "If Men Attended Fashion Shows as Women Do".... Now, Maxwell House takes pleasure in presenting one of MGM'S newest discoveries – Miss Christine Wells.... With Meredith Willson and his music, Miss Wells presents a special arrangement of melodies from Rudolph Friml's famous operatta – "Rose Marie".

ROSE MARIE MEDLEY
WELLS & ORCHESTRA

(APPLAUSE)

JESSEL: I thought that was lovely, Christine – good luck to you.

"HE WHO GETS SLAPPED"

JESSEL: Maxwell House now has the honor to present the second in our fall series in the M-G-M Theatre of the Air – Spencer Tracy and Rita Johnson in scenes from Andereyef's play, "He Who Get Slapped," specially adapted for radio. Music, Meredith – and curtain, please.

MUSIC: (UP AND FADE FOR:)

NARRATOR: "HE WHO GETS SLAPPED" is an immortal story, written by the great Russian, Andreyef. It is a story that is always old and always new, the story of a clown who laughs to hide his tears. The clown in our radio adaptation will be played by Spencer Tracy, but when the story begins he is not a clown. Until recently, he was a distinguished scientist – but fate has slapped him in the face and so he decided to follow a new profession. As our scene opens we find him, a gentleman in immaculate evening clothes, sitting in a box at the circus, long after the performance is over. The attendants are beginning to clean up the arena. One of them speaks to the magnificently dressed gentleman.

ATTENDANT: Staying all night, sir?

TRACY: No, of course not.

ATTENDANT: You'll have to go out through the back. The front of the house will be locked up.

TRACY:	Thank you. Where will I find the Manager's office?
ATTENDANT:	Through the door over there on your right.
TRACY:	There?
ATTENDANT:	Yes sir. There where those two clowns are just coming out.
TRACY:	Oh, yes.
MUSIC:	(COMES UP FOR A FEW SECONDS, THEN FADES UNDER THE FOLLOWING)
SOUND:	TWO MEN LAUGHING.
TRACY:	Excuse me.
CLOWN:	Yes sir. What can I do for you?
TRACY:	I see that you two gentlemen are clowns.
CLOWNS:	(TOGETHER) Yes sir.
TRACY:	A noble and enviable profession. May I shake hands with you?
CLOWNS:	(TOGETHER) You may, sir.
TRACY:	I am honored. And now, could you gentlemen show me the Manager's office?
CLOWNS:	That door right there.
TRACY:	Thank you. (PAUSE – KNOCKS ON DOOR)
BRIQUET:	(OFF) Come in (DOOR OPENS)
TRACY:	Pardon me. Would this be the Manager's office?

BRIQUET:	Yes sir. I am the Proprietor. What can I do for you?
TRACY:	Give me a chance to do something for you.
BRIQUET:	Oh, you want a job. You don't look like – well my friend, I can't afford extra talent.
TRACY:	But I don't expect to be paid anything to be a clown.
BRIQUET:	A clown! You? (LAUGHS) Well, well, what do you think of that? Jackson, come here.
JACKSON:	Yes, M'sieu.
BRIQUET:	This is the head clown of our circus, the famous Jim Jackson.
TRACY:	(ENTHUSIASTICALLY) I recognized him instantly. Even without his makeup. Oh, Mr. Jackson, you're a genius. You have given me such pleasure. Allow me to shake your hand.
JACKSON:	How are you?
BRIQUET:	Jackson, this gentleman wants to be a clown. Says he will work for nothing.
JACKSON:	No pay? That won't do. We have our Union. Let's see you grin. Like this.
TRACY:	How's that?
JACKSON:	Wider….broader….That's better. What else can you do?
TRACY:	I can be slapped.
	(BRIQUET AND JACKSON LAUGH)
BRIQUET:	That's no good. You see, my friend, clowns have to make the audience laugh.

TRACY:	They'll laugh when I'm slapped. They laughed when it happened before.
JACKSON:	You've clowned before, then?
TRACY:	Not – professionally.
BRIQUET:	(PATRONIZINGLY) But my friend, all clowns get slapped.
TRACY:	Yes, but they don't make speeches first.
BRIQUET:	Speeches!
TRACY:	Yes. About science. I know all about science, or art, philosophy… whatever you like.
JACKSON:	I'm beginning to see his idea. There's something about him like a scientist, a man of importance. Tell me, M'sieu, you impress them first by what you say. Is that right?
TRACY:	Yes. But can I say anything I please? Wise, important things?
JACKSON:	Sure, but we won't let you finish. One of the clowns will slap you down.
TRACY:	(BEAMING HAPPILY) Just what happens in the world outside. And people will call me "HE who gets slapped". (ALL LAUGHS)
JACKSON:	HE who gets slapped. Not bad.
TRACY:	And so I have found a name for myself, my friends. Call me HE.
JACKSON:	All right HE, try this.

SOUND:	SLAP
TRACY:	Wait a minute!
JACKSON:	HE who gets slapped. (EVERYBODY LAUGHS)
TRACY:	Why yes, of course. That's just the way it was.
BRIQUET:	(MYSTIFIED) The way it was?
TRACY:	Yes. It was funny, wasn't it? (LAUGHS)
MUSIC:	(UP AND FADES, AND OVER IT WE HEAR)
NARRATOR:	And so, this mysterious gentleman, HE who gets slapped becomes a clown. From the beginning HE is successful. HE insults his audiences and when HE is slapped, the people scream with laughter. But now, though no one knows it, HE has fallen in love. A beautiful young girl, the daughter of a penniless Italian Count has joined the troupe as a bareback rider, and from the first day HE has paid her delicate, scarcely noticeable attentions. But the beautiful Counsuelo would be the last to guess that HE is in love with her. Her heart belongs to Besano, the handsome young bareback rider who works with her in the ring. But she likes the clown, and one evening while the show is on, HE has just finished his act....
MUSIC:	("YE WHO HAVE YEARNED ALONE")
CONSUELO:	Congratulations HE. You were marvelous tonight.
TRACY:	Thank you.
CONSUELO:	But your costume. You poor dear! It's torn to pieces!
TRACY:	It always is when I come off.

CONSUELO:	You're forever doing things for me. Now I can do something for you. That beautiful red heart on your chest is about to fall off. Let me sew it on for you.
TRACY:	If it wouldn't be too much trouble....
CONSUELO:	No, no. Sit down here. It won't take a second...I saw you and Papa Briquet watching our act from the tunnel. You stand in the same place every night.
TRACY:	Beauty of form – beauty of line – beauty of rhythm.
CONSUELO:	Where did you learn such fancy speeches? HE, your mouth is so funny. Did you paint that laugh on yourself?
TRACY:	Yes, Consuelo.
CONSUELO:	I'd like to be a clown. Why are there no women clowns?
TRACY:	I really don't know.
CONSUELO:	Well, anyway, your heart won't come off again, when I've finished. But you must pay me for my work.
TRACY:	(LIGHTLY) With what? With my heart? Take it, it's yours.
CONSUELO:	How can I take it when I'm sewing it on? Tell my fortune. You said you would, sometime.
TRACY:	All right. Let me have your hand.
CONSUELO:	The last time it was a horrid old gypsy woman. HE, she said love would only come to me – through death. That makes no sense, does it?
TRACY:	Perhaps. But look there, see!
CONSUELO:	What?

TRACY:	The letter 'H'.
CONSUELO:	Yes, a sort of an 'H'.
TRACY:	'H' is for 'HE'.
CONSUELO:	(LAUGHS) Some 'he' always comes along, I suppose. Look again. See if you can't see a 'B'.
TRACY:	For Besano?
CONSUEO:	(A LITTLE FLUSTERED) Nonsense, HE.
TRACY:	(STILL TRYING TO BE LIGHT) No, there's no 'B'. If there were, it would mean 'Beware of bareback riders'... No – the 'H' is all I see.
CONSUELO:	(PROTESTING) HE, you haven't told me anything at all!
TRACY:	I've told you, but you didn't understand.
CONSUELO:	You'll have to be more plain. I'm not clever, you know. Don't jump like that, I might hurt you with the needle.
TRACY:	Consuelo, you are a crystal brook in the forest – that no man has drunk from – unstained, untouched. You must never know what it is to be false – to live a lie – to use your beauty to hurt, to do evil.
CONSUELO:	I still don't understand.
TRACY:	Youth turns to youth. Or youth stifles its urge to mate with beauty, and turns to – well, pearls, for instance, Consuelo.
CONSUELO:	I should like to have some pearls.

TRACY: Listen to me – there are deeper, more lovely things in life – that come only when we've lived long, and suffered. Pearls of the spirit – I have chests of jewels, Consuelo, to be poured out to enrich the woman I love!

CONSUELO: Why, HE, that's like something in a novel – and it's so funny, coming out of that face!

TRACY: I shall teach you to look behind the face. (PAUSE)

CONSUELO: 'H' for 'HE'. What did you mean?

TRACY: There's only one HE – a very old god who came down to earth only to love you – a goddess.

CONSUELO: What are you taking about, HE? Sometimes I think you're very wise, and what you say goes way over my head – and sometimes I think you're just a –

TRACY: (STUNG, VIOLENTLY) Fool? Consuelo, do you know that even gods can go crazy?

CONSUELO: Gods, go crazy? What are you talking about, HE? Listen!

MUSIC: (WE HAVE HEARD THE CIRCUS MUSIC FAINTLY. NOW IT BREAKS FORTH INTO A TEMPESTUOUS GALLOP)

CONSUELO: (RISING) Don't you know that music? It's Besano's solo ride. You never watch that, but I always do.

TRACY: Don't go! He is not for you!

CONSUELO: (DISTURBED) Why, HE, what's the matter?

TRACY: You're mine – you must be mine – the gods have said it – my soul sings your name, Consuelo – my love – my untouched – my pure in heart – my goddess, my queen.....

CONSUELO: Why – you – (SHE SLAPS HIM)

TRACY: Oh!

CONSUELO: (WITH REAL ANGER AND CONTEMPT) You make me feel sick all over. You forget who you are. What a god! Did the other gods slap you so hard that you fell out of heaven, god?

TRACY: Wait. Sit down. I – didn't finish the game.

CONSUELO: Was it a game? Why did you make me think you meant it, then?

TRACY: (LAUGHS) Slap me again!

CONSUELO: HE, I'm sorry I hit you. Now you're funny.

TRACY: Strike me again.

CONSUELO: I won't ever do that, HE.

TRACY: I want you to. It's part of – the game.

CONSUELO: (LAUGHS) There. Dear HE.

TRACY: I am the court fool, who loves his Queen. Didn't they teach you that every queen has a fool? HE Who Gets Slapped – if he presumes.

CONSUELO: But I'm not a Queen, foolish HE.

JESSEL: Meredith Willson and the boys pick it up from here with "I'm Going to Lock My Heart".

I'M GOING TO LOCK MY HEART
ORCHESTRA

(APPLAUSE)

"IF MEN ATTENDED FASHION SHOWS AS WOMEN DO"
TRACY-JESSEL-MORGAN-WILLSON

PEARSON: So many people have requested them, so here is another one of those Good News satires. This one is titled: "IF MEN ATTENDED FASHION SHOWS AS WOMEN DO." Frank Morgan and Spencer Tracy are just entering Meredith La Willson's Exclusive Tailor Salon to see the annual Fall Fashion Revue. They are met at the door by the famous fashion designer LA WILLSON, himself!

WILLSON: Hello there, Morgan…and Tracy!! My…it was certainly darling of you two to come.

MORGAN: I'm simply dying to see your new styles for fall. I'll bet they're scrumptious!

TRACY: I just need oodles of things, Willson…I really haven't a stitch to my back.

MORGAN: Are you going to show anything new in "undies?"

WILLSON: "Undies?" Well… just you wait till you feast your eyes on some of our new imported shorts and red-flannel longies. They're positively stunning.

TRACY: How about pajamas?? Do you think you might have anything with hiking boots to match? I walk in my sleep. Maybe some little thing in a beige-scarlet.

WILLSON: I'll see – but remind me later, Tracy. I have a monk's cloth lounging robe that would be a dream on you. (SIGHS) Oh…if I only had your figure…

TRACY: Well…you mustn't forget. In 1932 I was "Mr. Omaha."

WILLSON:	Excuse me a minute, boys... I have to see to some of my other customers. You know how it is when you're a big business man... (PROP LAUGH....FADES)
MORGAN:	Tracy...Don't you just hate giddy men? Always gig'ling...?
TRACY:	I'll say...And Willson of all people. He's beginning to look rather old, isn't he? Sort of dissipated like. He's getting circles under his circles...
MORGAN:	Yes...I think his schoolboy complexion is graduating.
TRACY:	Say, Morgan. Don't look now...but isn't that Georgie Jessel over there...??
MORGAN:	Where?
TRACY:	Over there...wearing that little fur hat with the flesh colored crown.
MORGAN:	Hat?? That's his head... he's getting bald!!
TRACY:	Oh, oh... he's seen us...and here he comes over here.
JESSEL:	(COMING UP) Hello, boys!! My... isn't this just ducky... running into you two like this?
MORGAN:	(ICE) Mmmmmm...
JESSEL:	And Tracy...What a perfectly precious snap-brim Adam Hat, with a two-color band. Do you mind if I try it on?
TRACY:	I really hate to take it off. My hair is a sight... but... here.
JESSEL:	Thanks, heaps. Mmm, I just wish I had a mirror here. How does it look on me, boys??
TRACY:	Adorable, Jessel. What do you think, Morgan?

MORGAN:	(ICE) Mmmmm….
JESSEL:	What's the matter, Morgan? Cat got your tongue?
MORGAN:	Jessel…You know good and well why I'm angry with you. Hmmm…having your tailor copy my blue herringbone-tweed cutaway.
JESSEL:	Well… the only reason I had it copied is because it looked so ravishing on you.
MORGAN:	Well… that's different. Mmmm, I DID look rather willowy in it, didn't I? But truthfully, Jessel… I thought you looked even better in it than I did…
JESSEL:	Yes…several other people said the same thing…
MORGAN:	No wonder they… WHAT?? Well what do they know?? After all, the original model was mine.
JESSEL:	That's no criterion. I've seen some lovely clothes worn by the wrong men….
MORGAN:	Listen here, you old copy-cat…
TRACY:	Boys…BOYS….QUIET!! The fashion show is starting.
WILLSON:	Welcome, men, and good afternoon – we start our show by presenting this outstanding garment for the tall… slender…soft-type of man. We call this our "Startled Fawn" number.
ALL:	Isn't it lovely?? OH's…Ah's…etc.
WILLSON:	This is a combination bathing suit and smoking jacket. Pure Angora wool with patch-pocket tobacco pouch cut on the bias. Just the thing for hopping into the pool with your favorite pipe. It's a steal for a measly hundred and seventy-nine dollars eighty-seven cents.

MORGAN:	Steal is right. It's practically highway robbery.
TRACY:	Yes… I think Willson charges too much for his things….
MORGAN:	You know what I do? I just remember the patterns of the outfits I like best…and then I have a little man who comes in and copies them for me on my own sewing machine. And for almost one third the cost.
TRACY:	Oh… you clever man.
WILLSON:	Now here is something youthful for evening. We call it our "First Date Thrill" number. Blue serge trimmed in olive green with white pearl buttons. A sort of semi-tuxedo.
TRACY:	The coat is rather chic but just look at those tight-fitting trousers with those high-water cuffs…Oh!
JESSEL:	High-water is right. If they were any higher his legs would be at half-mast. Say, Morgan – not changing the subject – but what is that bottle you're holding?
MORGAN:	It's a new kind of cologne…It's called "GHOST OF ROMANCE."
TRACY:	"Ghost of Romance??" It sounds fascinating.
MORGAN:	I use it mostly for after-shaving. It's so smoothy-cooly-comfy on your face-y…..Here…just let me put a few drops on your coat lapel.
JESSEL:	OH!!! MORGAN…YOU'RE SPILLING IT ALL OVER ME!!!
TRACY:	Say…what is that terrible odor??
JESSEL:	Phew – smells like a hospital.

MORGAN:	Let me see – Say – THE DRUGGIST GAVE ME THE WRONG BOTTLE… THIS ISN'T "GHOST OF ROMANCE…."
TRACY:	WHAT IS IT??
MORGAN:	SPIRITS OF CAMPHOR!!!
JESSEL:	OH…LET ME OUT OF HERE! I'VE GOT TO GET THESE CLOTHES OFF!!
	(MUSIC…..APPLAUSE)

(SECOND HALF OF SHOW)

EMCEE:	And now – Ted Pearson.
PEARSON:	Thanks – er, Meredith, mind joining us over here? Like to ask you a question.
MEREDITH:	Pray do.
PEARSON:	Meredith, how would you define freshness?
MEREDITH:	Why, I'd say, fresh as a new note in music.
PEARSON:	Fair enough – but you, Hanley? How would you define freshness?
STAFFORD:	Ted, I'd be pretty apt to steal your thunder and say fresh as Maxwell House Coffee.
PEARSON:	(LAUGHS) You're forgiven, Hanley. Yes … fresh as Maxwell House Coffee – for Maxwell House is roaster-fresh and no coffee can be fresher than that. And there's a big difference with coffee that's roaster-fresh and coffee that's not.

How many times have you gone into the grocery store and caught that appetizing smell of coffee? Many times, I suppose – but let me remind you again – that fragrance you smell is flavor escaping from coffee packed in ordinary containers…flavor being wasted. And that's flavor no one will ever get in the cup.

You see, all coffee, whether ground or the whole bean, starts to lose flavor the moment it's roasted. And ground coffee, packed in ordinary containers where the air can get at it, loses as much as forty-five per cent … nearly half its flavor … in only nine days.

But Maxwell House coffee is taken fresh and fragrant from the roasting ovens, and packed in that super-vacuum can from which all air is removed … and then sealed so no air can reach the coffee afterwards. You get it roaster-fresh. That means … full flavor in the cup.

So … if you haven't yet tried the new Maxwell House, by all means get a pound – it's the coffee you'll find now at all grocers in the same familiar blue super-vacuum can you've always known. And it's selling at low prices friendly to your budget. Try Maxwell House … tomorrow.

(MUSIC BRIDGE)

JESSEL: The doors of our imaginary haven, "The MGM Concert Hall" swing open and you are again invited to listen to a beautiful melody from the pen of a great composer. Meredith Willson pays tribute to the immortal Tchaikovsky in bringing you one of his most enchanting and gracious melodies…."The Sleeping Beauty".

"SLEEPING BEAUTY"
ORCHESTRA

(APPLAUSE)

FRANCIS WALLACE-GEORGE JESSEL

JESSEL: We present now, a special feature of tonight's program. A young man who is one of the country's foremost authorities on the national pastime for the fall – football. Here he is, ladies and gentlemen, Mr. Francis Wallace!

(APPLAUSE)

JESSEL: As I understand it, Frank, you're the fellow who crawled out on a limb in the Saturday Evening Post and predicted everything that was going to happen during the football season?

WALLACE: Right. I prepared a complete script. All the boys had to do was follow it.

JESSEL: And how's the script going?

WALLACE: Great – until last Saturday – when they started playing games. Either some of those boys can't read – or they're better jugglers than actors. So we had upsets.

JESSEL: What causes upsets?

WALLACE: We have more upsets in early-season games because the big teams are beginning to play each other early.

JESSEL: What about this week's games, Frank?

WALLACE: You mean you want my predictions?

JESSEL:	Of course. Being a master of ceremonies is all right but I'd like to make a few dollars on the side.
WALLACE:	Okay, Georgie. Here's a list of the games. You call 'em off and I'll predict 'em.
JESSEL:	All right…Here we go! Number one, Minnesota and Nebraska.
WALLACE:	Minnesota.
JESSEL:	Stanford and Santa Clara.
WALLACE:	Santa Clara.
JESSEL:	Ohio State – Indiana.
WALLACE:	Ohio State.
JESSEL:	Notre Dame and Kansas.
WALLACE:	Notre Dame – my alma mammy.
JESSEL:	Texas Christian versus Arkansas.
WALLACE:	Texas Christian.
JESSEL:	Auburn and Tulane.
WALLACE:	Auburn.
JESSEL:	That's my old Alma Mammy.
WALLACE:	Alabama, Polytechnic or Auburn, Georgia?
JESSEL:	Oh I thought that was Auburn Prison…Anyhow – who'll win the Columbia Yale game?
WALLACE:	Columbia.
JESSEL:	Louisiana State and Texas.

WALLACE: Louisiana State.

JESSEL: Wisconsin – Marquette?

WALLACE: Wisconsin.

JESSEL: Michigan and Michigan State.

WALLACE: Michigan.

JESSEL: North Carolina and North Carolina State.

WALLACE: North Carolina.

JESSEL: Two big states like that and they can't think up different names for the colleges…Oh, well – Rice and Oklahoma.

WALLACE: I'll take Rice.

JESSEL: I would too, but I'm on a diet. UCLA and Oregon.

WALLACE: UCLA.

JESSEL: The Pitt – Temple game.

WALLACE: I'll go for Pitt. Of course, most of those teams have not yet been tested under fire so don't be surprised at anything that happens anywhere.

JESSEL: Oh, sure – we don't expect you to give a written guarantee with these predictions but we all know, Frank, that if anybody'll come close it'll be you.

WALLACE: Thanks, Georgie. Remember those footballs still take fancy bounces.

JESSEL: Just a minute, Frank, before you go how about giving me that sixteen dollars you lost to me last week when you picked Southern Cal?

WALLACE:	Here you are, George.
JESSEL:	Thank you for coming, Frank. (APPLAUSE)
JESSEL:	Well…I guess it's about time for me to leave, too. I've really enjoyed being here this past hour and I'm grateful to Mr. Maxwell House for inviting me. However, before I go, allow me to remind you about getting your $250,000 quiz booklet at your favorite movie theatre. Remember this is motion pictures' greatest year. Next week your Good News show will be headed by Wallace Beery and Mickey Rooney doing scenes from Harry Rapf's great new picture "STABLEMATES". Bob Young will be back as Master of Ceremonies. Our special guest will be that fine comedian, sportsman and swell fellow… Joe E. Brown. Then of course there'll be the regular gang…Frank Morgan…Fannie Brice with Daddy Hanley Stafford…Phil Regan…Leni Lynn and Meredith Willson's music. All in all a typical grand Good News show, that you won't want to miss. In the meantime… go to the movies and take the family with you. This is Georgie Jessel saying…"Goodnight".
	("LAMBETH WALK" – FADES FOR)
PEARSON:	(MUSIC CREDITS)
	Flash! Good news for radio fans! Next Thursday evening Joe Penner returns to the air with Roy Atwell, Suzabella, and all the gang. Consult your paper for time and station and enjoy a fast half hour of fun and hilarity. A brand new show brought to you by General Foods on behalf of Huskies, the tempting new whole wheat breakfast cereal. Yes sir, Joe Penner will be back next Thursday night.

This is Ted Pearson bidding you goodnight for Maxwell House – the coffee that's good to the last drop….. This is the National Broadcasting Company.

Insomnia
(full script of Maxwell House Coffee Time, October 1, 1942

(ON CUE)

BRICE:	Daddy!
STAFF:	Snooks, please let me rest in my study. I want to finish this book.
BRICE:	Why do you always read books, Daddy?
STAFF:	Because I'm a bookworm.
BRICE:	Can you wiggle?
STAFF:	No, I can't wiggle!
BRICE:	Well, worms can wiggle.
STAFF:	A bookworm is a man who likes books!
BRICE:	Is a man who likes fish a fishworm?
STAFF:	Leave me alone! Why did you come in here, anyway?
BRICE:	I wanna get some water.
STAFF:	Water?
BRICE:	Yeah. My dolly just had a new baby and I wanna christen it.
STAFF:	Nonsense. You can't christen dolls with water.

BRICE: Why?

STAFF: Because it's only wax.

BRICE: Well, can I waxinate her?

STAFF: No! Just take your doll outside and play with it.

BRICE: She ain't got no clothes on.

STAFF: Well, find some in the closet. Wrap her up in one of mummy's smocks.

BRICE: Is a smock all right, daddy?

STAFF: A smock's swell.

BRICE: A smock's swell what?

STAFF: A smockswell house coffee time! Go away.

(APPLAUSE ... THEME)

HARLOW: Yes, ladies and gentlemen, it's Maxwell House Coffee Time, all right, and time once again for the delightful balderdash of Frank Morgan, the melodies of Meredith Willson and his orchestra, the tribulations of Hanley Stafford as Daddy, and the mischief of Fanny Brice as the one and only Baby Snooks! Now here is our master of ceremonies - your host for the evening - John Conte!

"EVERY NIGHT ABOUT THIS TIME"
CONTE & ORCH

(APPLAUSE)

CONTE: Thank you, ladies and gentlemen, and good evening. As some of you may know, tonight marks the beginning of National Newspaper Week. This network is saluting the men who bring you the printed news from the printer's devil all the way up to the publisher. We on this program would like to pay special tribute to the fourth estate by presenting the guiding spirit of the Los Angeles Daily News, a gentleman whose comforting voice has become known to millions of radio listeners thru his brilliant and comprehensive analyses of vital topics. Ladies and gentlemen, the editor and publisher of the Daily News – Mr. Manchester Boddy. Mr. Boddy.

(APPLAUSE)

BODDY: Thank you.

CONTE: Mr. Boddy, since you are a member of the American Society of Newspaper Editors, and working publisher of one of Los Angeles' biggest dailies, would you care to make a statement with regard to the significance of National Newspaper Week?

BODDY: Indeed I would, John. But since this program is only on for thirty minutes, I'm afraid I'd leave too much unsaid.

CONTE: You mean the subject couldn't be covered in less than thirty minutes?

BODDY: It probably could – but not by me. I'm the talkingest man on the West Coast.

CONTE: Well, I've heard you on the air – and you can keep talking for my money. So far, everything you've said has made sense.

BODDY: Unfortunately, I'm not impervious to flattery – so you can expect a complimentary year's subscription starting tomorrow.

MERE: Well, I guess that's what you call a free press.

(LAUGHS) You know, get it for nothing. (LAUGHS SOME MORE) Oh, boy.

CONTE: Oh. This is Meredith Willson, Mr. Boddy. Our maestro.

BODDY: I'm delighted to meet you, Mr. Willson. My paper has covered most of your concerts – and I can truthfully say that Meredith Willson occupies a prominent position in our morgue.

MERE: Huh?

CONTE: Don't be alarmed, Meredith – in newspaper jargon the morgue is another name for the files.

MERE: Oh. Well, you got a great little paper there, Mr. Boddy. Yes sir. I and Peggy – that's –er- Mrs. Willson – we fight for it over the breakfast table every morning.

BODDY: Really? Who gets it?

MERE: The cook, most of the time. I never squawk because you know how hard it is to get help these days, and if you're lucky —

CONTE: Okay, okay. Mr. Boddy didn't come here to listen to your servant problem, Meredith.

BODDY: On the contrary, John. I'm deeply interested in it. Do you have a good cook now, Mr. Willson?

MERE: Oh, pretty fair, I guess. I eat almost anything – Peggy's the fancy one. But we do our best to please the cook.

BODDY: Isn't that the truth? And how long has she been with you?

MERE: With us? She's been against us ever since she came.

CONTE:	Mr. Boddy, may I remind you that your appearance on this program was to stimulate interest in National Newspaper Week?
BODDY:	Are you serious, Jockey?
CONTE:	Mr. Boddy!
BODDY:	Do you think for one moment that I'm naïve enough to believe that's the reason you asked me to come here this evening?
CONTE:	Well – would I ask you for any other reason?
BODDY:	Certainly. Frank Morgan has to have somebody to push around, doesn't he?
MERE:	Now, just a minute, Mr. Boddy. Frank wouldn't think of kidding with a man of your importance!
BODDY:	Well, if he doesn't, I'll feel highly insulted. And John, if you think the listeners would like to understand the significance of National Newspaper Week – I suggest they consult their local newspapers first thing in the morning.
CONTE:	A good idea. Now, Mr. Boddy, I'm going to ask you a question that's been asked a thousand times. Do you think the radio will ever replace the newspaper?
BODDY:	John, I'm going to give you the answer that's been given just as often. Radio will never replace the newspaper.
CONTE:	Why not?

BODDY: Because you can't wrap a sandwich in a radio. Seriously, though, radio and the newspaper industry no longer consider each other competitors. It's like the Army and the Navy – both use different methods in accomplishing their missions – but they both serve a common cause.

MERE: Gee, this is interesting. Mr. Boddy, do you see everything before it's printed in your paper?

BODDY: Just about.

MERE: I wonder if you'd clear up something that's been worrying me for several days. I hate to ask you this – but I know you like to keep the people informed on vital stuff —

BODDY: Don't hesitate, my boy. I'll be glad to answer it if I can.

MERE: Well – (STALLS)

CONTE: Go on, Meredith – if it's such a pressing question – ask him.

MERE: Okay. Mr. Boddy – how is Superman gonna get away from the Monocle?

CONTE: Get out of here, you lunkhead! Superman. How do you like that?

BODDY: Confidentially, it's got me worried, too. I can't imagine what's going to happen to Race Riley, either.

CONTE: Do you actually find time to read the funnies?

BODDY: First page I turn to. Don't you like them?

CONTE: Well, since we're all letting our hair down – that's all I ever read. And if there's one thing I like, it's to see that Dixie Dugan strip.

MORGAN:	(COMING ON) Well, I'd like to see it, too! What time does she start peeling?
CONTE:	Frank!
	(APPLAUSE)
MORGAN:	Hello, fellows. Is this Dixie dame as good as Lolita in the Main Street Follies?
BODDY:	Mr. Morgan, the Dixie Dugan strip is not calculated to stir the baser emotions. It's comic.
MORGAN:	(COLDLY) Oh, it is? Well, I suppose when I get to be your age, I'll find it funny, too. But right now I find it exhilarating . . . Who's this anemic looking fink, Jockey?
CONTE:	Fink!
MERE:	He's no frink, Fank!
MORGAN:	Frinkfank?
CONTE:	Frank – this is the man who's responsible for your receiving your Los Angeles Daily News every morning!
MORGAN:	He is! Well, listen to me, son, I want you to place that paper on my doorstep instead of tossing it in the shrubbery as you go by on your bike! I'm sick and tired of stepping in —
MERE:	Jeepers, Frank! He doesn't deliver the papers on a bicycle!
MORGAN:	No?
BODDY:	No, Mr. Morgan. I work downtown.

MORGAN: Not really! Say, tell me – how do you lads stand between the cars at all the intersections without getting your brains knocked out?

CONTE: Stop it, you lunatic! This gentleman is not a newspaper vendor, nor is he a carrier, Pigeon!

MORGAN: Oh, carrier pigeon. I thought you told me he works for the Los Angeles Daily News.

CONTE: He does!

BODDY: That's right.

MORGAN: Well, you needn't be so proud of it, son. If I ever saw a yellow journal – that's it! I can't imagine why the editor hasn't been run out of town on a rail.

MERE: (WORRIED) Oh, Frank —

MORGAN: And as for the publisher, I can't find words enough to express my disgust about a man who would allow such sordid —

CONTE: Frank! Do you know what you're saying?

MORGAN: Wrong thing?

CONTE: This is the editor and publisher of that paper – Manchester Boddy!

MORGAN: Ohh – err – bogey man . . . Chestnuts . . . Now I know how the dragon felt when he met the good knight, St. George. Goodnight, George.

CONTE: Come back here, Morgan! You owe Mr. Boddy an apology!

MORGAN: (INDIGNANTLY) I – well of all – do you mean – well, what are you waiting for, Meredith?

MERE: Please, Mr. Boddy, accept my humble apology for the misunderstanding – it was all my fault and I want to thank you from the bottom of my heart – and Mr. Morgan's bottom, too. (LIP TREMBLES) Is that all right, Frank?

MORGAN: No, it was too toadying! And if you expect Mr. Bogey to swallow that kind of —

BODDY: Boddy.

MORGAN: You just stay out of it, son. I'm ashamed of you, Meredith – you may go.

MERE: I'm sorry, Frank.

MORGAN: Poor boy's suffering from a case of arrested development. I'm trying to develop him before he gets arrested. Well, I have to be —

CONTE: No, you don't! Not until you make amends to our guest!

BODDY: That's all right, John. We still have free speech in this country, and if Mr. Morgan doesn't like my newspaper he has a perfect right —

MORGAN: Like your newspaper! My dear Mr. Catboat —

BODDY: Boddy.

MORGAN: Yes. Surely a man of your culture and great journalistic talents can appreciate a little joke!

CONTE: A little joke!

MORGAN: Certainly. (I wish I could think of one and change the subject.)

CONTE: Don't let him get away with it, Mr. Boddy. He embarrasses everybody who appears on this program, and I'm tired of it!

MORGAN: (BRIDLING) That's an infamous bit of truth-juggling! And I can prove that your slip is entirely without foundation, Corset! (I thought those were unmentionables.)

BODDY: Well, let's just forget about it. If you have any suggestions that'll improve my paper, I'll be very glad to hear them.

MORGAN: Well, I'd hesitate to offer any, Mr. Boneyard —

BODDY: Boddy!

MORGAN: Yes. You see, journalism has changed a good deal since I won my spurs as a star reporter on the now defunct Peapack Herald. But I might —

CONTE: Hold it! You know something about the newspaper business?

MORGAN: (LAUGHS) Are you serious, Jockey? The Morgans have been newsmen for generations, beginning with my grandfather, Linotype Morgan, down to my Uncle Scarehead and my Aunt Column.

BODDY: Your Aunt Column?

MORGAN: A very upright woman. But she had her peculiar leanings. My shrewd aunt dictated the editorial policy of the paper, and soon took it from a barely-paying two page affair into a colossal thirty page bankruptcy.

CONTE: Pretty shrewd.

MORGAN: In a microcephalic sort of a way. She was the original sob-sister, but her sobbing had no effect on the judge and he wouldn't grant her request to occupy the same cell as my uncle. My poor gaffer couldn't get rid of the journalistic itch – so he decided to start from scratch again.

BODDY: Wasn't that a little rash?

MORGAN: Oh – rash!

MERE: Can I come back now, Frank?

MORGAN: Where have you been?

MERE: I had to leave because you insulted Mr. Boddy.

MORGAN: Oh. Well, stick around and maybe you can insult him when I want to leave. Where was I?

CONTE: Scratching your gaffer's rash.

MORGAN: Yes. We tried calamine lotion and that didn't seem to— wait a minute!

MERE: Don't mix him up, John! Frank, you were telling us how you started a newspaper with your grandfather.

MORGAN: Thank you, Meredith. We had to overcome many obstacles in the beginning, but we were Morgans – and it's traditional that every member of our family lives and dies by the noose. News!

BODDY: Did you run a liquor campaign?

MORGAN: Yes – but nobody sent us any so we killed it after the second edition. We tried every circulation-getting feature known to journalism – but with no success. We literally starved during those days – and my poor gaffer became a pitiful figure of a man, wan and pale, and his trousers in tatters. I knew his end was in sight.

MERE: Couldn't you get a scoop, Frank?

MORGAN: It seemed impossible. But fortune was to smile upon us very soon. It was Christmas day, and I was sitting quietly at my desk reading the life of Horace Greeley – when suddenly the phone rang. I was instantly galvanized into action. I said, "Hello".

CONTE: Hello!

MORGAN: Will you please call Betty to the – No! I warn you, Jockey, I won't tolerate any more of those interruptions!

CONTE: Well, I won't tolerate any more of your fantastic lies!

MORGAN: Philistine! I'm getting out of here!

MERE: Oh, don't go – please, Frank!

MORGAN: No! I'm not going to stand for such slipshod slurs slid from the slot of a shabby snob! (I'd like to have a recording of that.)

BODDY: Mr. Morgan, I'm fascinated by your story. Please finish it.

MORGAN: All right. As soon as I answered the phone I knew I had a scoop. A voice at the other end informed me that a horse had run away with the madcap daughter of Peapack's richest banker!

CONTE:	What kind of a scoop is that? A horse runs away with an heiress?
MORGAN:	Well, how would you like to have a horse for a son-in-law? I dashed out to the banker's mansion, hastily disguised myself as a butcher, and was admitted at the tradesman's entrance.
BODDY:	How did you manage to disguise yourself as a butcher, Mr. Morgan?
MORGAN:	I pulled out my shirt tails, grabbed a lamp chop from the watchdog, and borrowed a straw hat from a passerby.
CONTE:	A straw hat? Christmas day?
MORGAN:	The man was an eccentric. Once I was in the kitchen, I spent two hours with the buxom scullery maid – getting facts, of course –
CONTE:	Of course.
MORGAN:	Of course.
MERE:	Of course.
MORGAN:	I – oh. It turned out the story was a hoax, but I got a better one from the scullery maid. (GIGGLES) I knew it would ruin the banker – but a scoop's a scoop – and I needed it badly.
BODDY:	What was the story?
MORGAN:	It was incredible! I dashed back to the office –
CONTE:	Was it about his love life?

MORGAN: Worse than that. I got to the composing room, wrote the thing in type, went to set a headline over it in 88 point Gothic – and found there was a paucity of uppercase letters.

CONTE: Paucity of uppercase letters – what's that?

MORGAN: No caps.

CONTE: Oh, well, I'll take a derby.

MORGAN: Sweatband?

CONTE: Just a sponge.

MORGAN: That'll be four dollars and – what are we talking about!

MERE: You cut that out, John! Go on, Frank.

CONTE: Well, he won't tell us what the story was about the banker.

MORGAN: Well, it's too complicated.

BODDY: If you don't tell us, I won't sleep tonight.

MORGAN: Very well. I'll tell you the weirdest story of a man that was ever printed. This banker had married a widow with a grown daughter. Then the banker's father married the grown daughter – and that made him the banker's son-in-law.

MERE: Uh-huh.

MORGAN: It also made the banker's step-daughter his mother – because she was his father's wife. Soon the banker and his wife had a son, which became his father's brother-in-law, and his own uncle, since he was the brother of his step-mother. His father's wife had a son, too – who, of

	course, was the banker's brother, and also his grandchild because he was the son of his daughter.
BODDY:	Hmmmmm.
MORGAN:	Accordingly, the banker's wife was his grandmother because she was his mother's mother. He was his wife's husband and grandchild at the same time – and as the husband of a person's grandmother is his grandfather – the banker was his own grandfather! If you find a better scoop than that – let me know. So long, fellers!

(MUSIC ... APPLAUSE)

MIDDLE COMMERCIAL

WILCOX:	Y'know, John ... music's wonderful!
CONTE:	Especially the way Meredith's boys dish it out, Harlow.
MERE:	(MIFFED) "Dish" it, he says! I'll have you understand they *render* it ... interpret the soul, the feeling, the ...
CONTE:	Yes - yes, I know, Meredith. My apologies.
MERE:	Wel-l-l ... all right, John. (BRIGHTLY) But we sure *can* tear off some mean harmony, at that!
WILCOX:	What can you do with a *sonata*?
MERE:	Jeepers, Harlow – a sonata's an instrumental composition of three or four movements in different, though related, keys... and in different forms and moods. Usually a *solo* number.
CONTE:	So you're stuck when it comes to an *orchestral* rendition, eh?

MERE:	Who says we're stuck? Hey Ralph... unwind a few bars of Ludwig Beethoven's "Moonlight Sonata", opus twenty-seven, Number two.
	(NOTE TO MEREDITH: THIS TIME IT'S YOUR CHOICE. PLAY WHATEVER YOU CAN BREAK DOWN INTO THE FOUR PASSAGES NEEDED FOR COFFEE-BLENDING PARALLEL TO FOLLOW)
	(PIANO... FEW BARS TO IDENTIFY TUNE)
WILCOX:	Isn't that lovely? Say, can you *orchestrate* that part?
MERE:	Certainly. As the piano continues, we add woodwinds for mellowness –
	(ORCHESTRA: WOODWINDS WITH PIANO... ENOUGH BARS FOR EFFECT)
	Next, the strings lend richness...
	(ORCHESTRA: STRINGS WITH OTHERS AS DIRECTED)
	Then the brasses give body...
	(ORCHESTRA: BRASSES WITH OTHERS AS DIRECTED)
	And the rhythm section provides vigor...
	(FULL ORHCESTRA: AS DIRECTED)
	See what I mean, Harlow? My boys can *dish it out*!
	(CATCHES HIMSELF) Er... I mean, *render*...
WILCOX:	(LAUGHS) Whatever the term, that was a swell job

of musical moonlight. Now, if I may, I'll contribute a *solo* in a "different though related *key*" as you said when describing a sonata.

(START COMMERCIAL TIME HERE. 153 WORDS, 53 SECONDS, PLUS 16 SECONDS MUSIC)

WILCOX: *My* key, friends is *coffee* ... specifically, how the Maxwell House people *blend* highland-grown, extra-flavor coffees from Latin America – to give you "moonlight in a cup".

Now moonlight is mellow – so for *mellowness,* Maxwell House uses magnificent Manizales ...

(ORCHESTRA: WOODWINDS WITH PIANO AS BEFORE ... FOUR SECONDS)

For *richness,* choice Medellins ...

(ORHCESTRA: STRINGS WITH OTHERS AS BEFORE ... FOUR SECONDS)

For full body, exquisite Bucaramangas ...

(ORCHESTRA: BRASSES WITH OTHERS AS BEFORE ... FOUR SECONDS)

WILCOX: And for *vigorous, winy* flavor – Central and South America ... (FULL ORCHESTRA AS BEFORE ... FOUR SECONDS)

So – with *each* of these prime coffees imparting its *own* characteristic qualities to the superb Maxwell House blend ... well, how *can* it be otherwise than wonderfully rich and delicious? You're right – Maxwell House is *all* of that and then some ... yes, the largest-selling vacuum-packed coffee in the world!

And while such premium coffees naturally cost *us* more, Maxwell House costs *you* but a fraction of a cent more per cup than even the *cheapest* coffees!

These days it pays to get *good* coffee... Maxwell House Coffee... now, as always... Good to the Last *Drop*!

(PLAY-OFF)

CONTE: That was swell, Meredith. And now, ladies and gentle —

STAFF: (TIRED) Hello, John.

CONTE: Why, daddy! You look exhausted.

STAFF: Haven't slept a wink. Three nights now.

CONTE: Are you pacing with the twins?

STAFF: No – I can't blame the children for this. I've got insomnia in its worst form.

CONTE: Oh, that's too bad. Have you seen a doctor?

STAFF: Yes. He gave me some sleeping tablets and told me to eat very lightly before retiring. Last night I went to bed around eleven o'clock and started tossing. I decided to go down into the kitchen for a glass of warm milk before trying a sleeping tablet and – (FADES)

(SNOOKS PLAY-ON)

FATHER: I guess I ought to nibble on something light while the milk is boiling... (OPENS ICE BOX)... Hmmm – something light. This looks good.

BRICE: Hello, daddy.

FATHER: Snooks! (ICE BOX CLOSES) What are you doing out of bed at this time of night?

BRICE: The sheet slipped off.

FATHER: Well, couldn't you put it back on the bed?

BRICE: No. I got out to tuck myself in – and I wasn't there.

FATHER: Well, go back and look for yourself – and stay there.

BRICE: Why?

FATHER: Because I don't like to see you standing here in your nightie?

BODDY: Shall I take it off?

FATHER: No – just go to your room and go to sleep!

BRICE: I ain't sleepy, daddy.

FATHER: Well, I am!

BRICE: Then why don't you go to sleep?

FATHER: Because I've got insomnia. I can't sleep. I haven't closed my eyes for three nights.

BRICE: Maybe that's why you can't sleepy, daddy. If you close your —

FATHER: I close my eyes – but they won't stay closed! And I can't stay in bed.

BRICE: Why?

FATHER: I told you, I have insomnia! It's a nervous disorder which produces abnormal wakefulness, due to a psychological stimuli and sometimes brings about a complete maladjustment of the neurological fibers.

BRICE: Imagine that.

FATHER: Now do you know why I can't stay in bed?

BRICE: Uh-huh – mummy kicked you out.

FATHER: She did not! Mummy has nothing to do with my condition.

BRICE: Well, who done it?

FATHER: Nobody. It comes on suddenly – and they haven't found an adequate cure for it yet. I've tried deep breathing, relaxing, counting sheep – nothing helps.

BRICE: Have you tried sleeping?

FATHER: Certainly I have. But that's the point – if you have insomnia you can't sleep.

BRICE: I can sleep.

FATHER: Well, I wish you would. Goodnight.

BRICE: What are you gonna do, daddy?

FATHER: I'm going to try the doctor's suggestion. He said a light snack might do the trick.

BRICE: Do you want some ketchup for them pork chops?

FATHER: No thanks, I won't eat them all, anyway. Just two or three, and a piece of cold lamb – possibly a couple of potatoes, but that's all.

BRICE: What about that pickle, daddy?

FATHER: I don't know. I'm not certain whether I can keep it on my stomach all night.

BRICE: I bet it'll roll off.

FATHER: I mean digest it. Oh, I don't suppose it'll hurt. Look out, Snooks.

BRICE: Why are you putting those beans away, daddy?

FATHER: A man can't make a pig of himself. (ICE BOX OPENS AND CLOSES) There, I guess the milk's just about ready, too. Take it off the stove, Snooks.

BRICE: Can I drink some?

FATHER: Sure – drink it all. I'll take some cold beer.

BRICE: I want some beer.

FATHER: Snooks!

BRICE: I want some beer!

FATHER: Beer is not for children! The only reason I'm drinking it is because it might have a sedative effect on me.

BRICE: You drink it all day.

FATHER: Well – I've got to kill this case of insomnia!

BRICE: You killed the case of beer, too.

FATHER: That's none of your business! You've never seen me touch the stuff until I got this attack, have you?

BRICE: No, daddy.

FATHER: Well, all right. It's bitter medicine and I only take it on doctor's orders. (SILLY LAUGH) Go to bed.

BRICE: Goodnight, daddy.

FATHER: Goodnight.

BRICE: Daddy?

FATHER:	Yes?
BRICE:	Can I get married?
FATHER:	Not tonight.
BRICE:	Why?
FATHER:	It's too cold.
BRICE:	Can I get married tomorrow?
FATHER:	If it gets warmer.
BRICE:	Was it warm when you got married?
FATHER:	No – but your mummy's made it hot for me ever since. Goodnight.
BRICE:	Goodnight, daddy... Daddy?
FATHER:	What is it?
BRICE:	I wanna help you go to sleep, my sweet little daddy.
FATHER:	How can you help me go to sleep?
BRICE:	I'll let you do my homework. It always makes me go to sleep.
FATHER:	You mean to say you haven't done your homework for tomorrow?
BRICE:	I ain't even done it for yesterday.
FATHER:	Snooks, how can you hope to get educated if you don't pay attention to your work? Haven't you learned anything in school this year?
BRICE:	I learned to be very polite, daddy. I learned to say "Yes sir" and "No sir" and "Yes ma'am" and "No ma'am."

FATHER:	You did?
BRICE:	Yeah.
FATHER:	Well, I can see you forgot it in a hurry. What's your homework for tomorrow?
BRICE:	Gozinter.
FATHER:	Gozinter?
BRICE:	Yeah – two gozinter four – four gozinter eight –
FATHER:	That's division! What's your first problem?
BRICE:	My first problem is where's my homework?
FATHER:	What do you mean? Didn't the teacher give you the questions written on paper?
BRICE:	Yeah – but it got tore up.
FATHER:	How did it get torn up?
BRICE:	When I was making spitballs to clunk my teacher on the head.
FATHER:	Clunk her!
BRICE:	Yeah – clunk her.
FATHER:	Snooks, I don't believe it! You wouldn't have the audacity to throw spitballs at your teacher! You wouldn't!
BRICE:	Wouldn't I?
FATHER:	Oh, you're helping me go to sleep all right! This'll keep me awake for another week!
BRICE:	I'm sorry, daddy.

FATHER: I'll talk to you about it in the morning. It's way past midnight now – so you'd better go to bed.

BRICE: Are you getting sleepy?

FATHER: No.

BRICE: Well, would you like to help me with yesterday's homework?

FATHER: Oh, all right. Get your stuff and let's go to the bedroom. It might put me to sleep. Let me bring my sleeping tablets.

BRICE: What are they for, daddy?

FATHER: To cure my insomnia. I've already taken nine – and I'm supposed to take another one at one o'clock.

BRICE: I'll remind you.

FATHER: Okay. Where's your homework? Is this it?

BRICE: Uh-huh.

FATHER: Hmmmm . . . let's see how many of these questions you can answer by yourself. Got a pencil and paper?

BRICE: Uh-huh.

FATHER: All right. First question – what's the shape of the earth?

BRICE: Flat.

FATHER: We're not talking about its condition – just the shape. The earth is not flat. Now, what shape is it?

BRICE: Round.

FATHER: How do you know it's round?

BRICE:	All right, then – it's square – I don't wanna fight.
FATHER:	Good enough for me. Put down square. Second question. Can you tell in ten words or less what the equator is? Can you?
BRICE:	Uh-huh.
FATHER:	Are you sure?
BRICE:	Uh-huh.
FATHER:	Well, what is the equator?
BRICE:	I dunno.
FATHER:	I thought so. The equator is an imaginary line that runs around the earth. Imaginary means non-existent – nothing. Put that down.
BRICE:	I got it.
FATHER:	You got what? I didn't see you write anything.
BRICE:	Well, you told me the answer is nothing – so I didn't put down nothing.
FATHER:	The answer is not nothing – it's something. The nothing I mentioned to you wasn't anything, but it's something because it explains that nothing is part of the answer of the something that you put down nothing for.
BRICE:	Are you getting sleepy, daddy?
FATHER:	No – I'm wide awake! Write down that the equator is an imaginary line running around the earth, everywhere equally distant from the two poles and dividing the earth's surface into two hemispheres. Got that?

BRICE:	Uh-huh. Is that two "F's" in hemisphere?
FATHER:	One F! Put it down! Here's the next question. Australia has a very damp climate. What do they raise there?
BRICE:	Umbrellas.
FATHER:	No – sheep! Australia produces more sheep than any other country in the world. Name the members of the sheep family.
BRICE:	Robespierre, Pluto, Hibiscus –
FATHER:	Those are my kids! They're not sheep! What's the father sheep called?
BRICE:	Daddy.
FATHER:	It's called a ram. The mother sheep is ewe.
BRICE:	Me?
FATHER:	Not me – ewe!
BRICE:	Is you the sheep's mummy?
FATHER:	Yes – ewe is the sheep's mummy.
BRICE:	Well, is it me or you?
FATHER:	It's neither of us! It's ewe – E-W-E!
BRICE:	Oh, eeeweeee.
FATHER:	The daddy sheep is called a ram, the mummy is ewe and the lamb is the baby. Put it down.
BRICE:	I got it.
FATHER:	What have you got?
BRICE:	You're the mummy, ram the daddy and lam the baby.

FATHER:	You'll really mop up with this homework. Sign your name to it and go to sleep. I'm getting drowsy. (YAWNS) Must be those sheep.
BRICE:	See, I told you my homework would do it, daddy.
FATHER:	Uh-huh. I'll lie here on the couch. Goodnight.
BRICE:	Goodnight, daddy.
FATHER:	Hmmmm... (SETTLES)... Ahhhhhh.
BRICE:	(SOFTLY) Daddy?
FATHER:	Yes?
BRICE:	Will you tell me a sleepy little story?
FATHER:	Sure. There was once a man who had insomnia and he didn't sleep for three nights. So his little girl asked him to help her with his homework and he did. Then he – got --- very ---- sleepy ---- (SNORES) - - -
BRICE:	(GETTING SLEEPY) Uh-huh.
FATHER:	(ALMOST ASLEEP) And he – was – so happy when – sleep finally – came ---- (SNORES FOR A FEW SECONDS) (CLOCK CHIMES ONCE)
BRICE:	(HOLLERS) Daddy!
FATHER:	What's the matter? I was fast asleep.
BRICE:	It's one o'clock!
FATHER:	Well, what of it?
BRICE:	It's time to take your sleeping tablet!

FATHER:	Ohhhhh – you little --- (WHACK)
BRICE:	Waaaahhhhhhh!
	(MUSIC . . . APPLAUSE)

CLOSING COMMERCIAL

CONTE:	Say, boys – have you thought about going on a diet?
MERE:	Jeepers, no . . . not me. I don't need to reduce.
WILCOX:	Me neither, John. Why do you ask?
CONTE:	Well, it looks like we're scheduled for shorter rations – in *some* directions.
MERE:	Shucks . . . we can't go any farther west – let's go east!
CONTE:	(LAUGHS) Be sensible, Meredith! I simply meant that certain foods will soon be rationed. For instance, we may not be able to buy as much *meat* as usual.
WILCOX:	Yes, I hear each person will get around two and a half pounds per week.
MERE:	How does that figure at dinner time . . . say, *two* pork chops instead of *three*?
WILCOX:	Dunno, Meredith. But that's about the right portion for something *else* folks like mighty well.
CONTE:	What's that, pray tell?
	(START COMMERCIAL TIME HERE . . . 198 WORDS, 1 MINUTE, 8 SECONDS)

WILCOX: *Coffee*! Y'see, friends, coffee isn't exactly *plentiful* anymore ... just can't import as much ... so maybe we'll have to make *two* cups do for *three*, as an average reduction. That goes for Maxwell House, too. But we're doing our best to supply food stores with as much Maxwell House as possible. Even so, you may be unable to get it *every* time you shop. But ask for it just the same – so you won't miss a single opportunity to take home truly *good* coffee.

WILCOX: For now as always, Maxwell House gives you an extra measure of extra-flavor, Latin-American coffees ... perfectly blended. Furthermore, Maxwell House is already precisely ground for your favorite brewing method. Be careful of *that*, because you'll want *full* flavor, strength and enjoyment from *every* pound of Maxwell House Coffee you buy.

Just follow the directions you'll find printed on the Maxwell House label. Figure how many cups you'll need ... make no more than you'll drink ... measure coffee and water exactly. That's how to get the best in Maxwell House Coffee flavor – economically, too – no matter which method you prefer.

So if you really "go" for truly *good* coffee, ask your grocer tomorrow for ... *Maxwell House Coffee*!

(EASTERN BROADCAST *ONLY*)

THEME ... FADES FOR:

CONTE: Well, that minute hand on the clock tells me it's time to say goodnight, ladies and gentlemen, but we'll all be back next Thursday evening at Maxwell House Coffee Time.

Fanny Brice as Baby Snooks, Frank Morgan, who appears with us through the courtesy of Metro-Goldwyn-Mayer, Hanley Stafford, Meredith Willson and his orchestra, and Harlow Wilcox.

Maxwell House Coffee Time is written by Phil Rapp.

This is John Conte, saying goodnight and good luck from the makers of Maxwell House – the coffee that is always – Good to the Last Drop!

(REPEAT SHOW ONLY)

THEME ... FADES FOR:

CONTE: Well, that minute hand on the clock tells me it's time to say goodnight, ladies and gentlemen, but we'll all be back next Thursday evening at Maxwell House Coffee Time.

Fanny Brice as Baby Snooks, Frank Morgan, who appears with us through the courtesy of Metro-Goldwyn-Mayer, Hanley Stafford, Meredith Willson and his orchestra, and Harlow Wilcox.

Maxwell House Coffee Time is written by Phil Rapp.

Oh, incidentally, don't miss Hal Burdick and his famous "Night Editor" stories ... fifteen minutes of grand entertainment... presented over many of these stations every Thursday immediately before Maxwell House Coffee Time.

And this is John Conte, saying goodnight and good luck from the makers of Maxwell House – the coffee that is always – Good to the Last Drop!

If your folks fail to agree on *which* cereal they prefer, get them *Post-Tens*... the "please-everybody" package for hard-to-please families. Yes, only *one* package – but *five* of America's favorite cereals... Post Toasties, Post's Forty Per Cent Bran Flakes, Grape-Nuts, Grape-Nuts Flakes, Nabisco Shredded Wheat. Post-Tens contain *individual* boxes of each delicious cereal – ten wrapped together in cellophane. So remember, folks – for whole-grain nourishment every day, pick and choose the *Post-Tens* way!

THIS IS THE NATIONAL BROADCASTING COMPANY.

Homework
(February 15, 1940)

MAXWELL HOUSE
2-15-40

ARNOLD: And now, ladies and gentlemen, here is Fanny Brice as Baby Snooks!

(MUSIC....APPLAUSE)

ARNOLD: Tonight, Daddy, played by Hanley Stafford, is in an awful dither. The tax returns for his firm must be made out and he finds his books are not in order. As the scenes opens, Daddy is working on his accounts - trying to make them balance before the boss comes to pick them up. Listen...

FATHER: This can't be right....Shortage of over three thousand dollars... Hmmm... Better check those assets again.

BRICE: Hello, daddy.

FATHER: Hmm! I'm looking for assets and in walks a liability!

BRICE: Huh?

FATHER: Nothing. Snooks, I must ask you to leave this room at once.

BRICE: Why?

FATHER:	Because I want to be alone.
BRICE:	(LAUGHS) Say it again, daddy.
FATHER:	I want to be alone.
BRICE:	(LAUGHS)
FATHER:	What are you laughing at?
BRICE:	You sound like Greta Garbage.
FATHER:	Never mind that! I've important work to do and I demand absolute privacy!
BRICE:	What are you doing, daddy?
FATHER:	You can see I'm up to my ears in charts and figures! That only means one thing.
BRICE:	You're dopin' the horses.
FATHER:	I'm not doing anything of the kind! I'm trying to get my books back in shape!
BRICE:	Those big square ones?
FATHER:	Yes!
BRICE:	What shape was they before?
FATHER:	(BARKS) Round with frilled edges! (MAD LAUGH)
BRICE:	(LAUGHS) Waaaahhhh!
FATHER:	Now, don't start anything, Snooks. I feel bad!
BRICE:	Why?
FATHER:	Because I just discovered an enormous discrepancy in my assets.

BRICE:	Let me see it, daddy.
FATHER:	You can't see it! It's nothing you can put your finger on.
BRICE:	Does it hurt that much?
FATHER:	It'll ruin me if I don't find it.
BRICE:	Ain't you found it yet?
FATHER:	No.
BRICE:	Then how do you know you got it?
FATHER:	I just looked on my debit side and found an increment.
BRICE:	Let me put my finger on it.
FATHER:	Don't be silly. It's the growth on my debit side that's causing the hole on my credit side.
BRICE:	You're really sick, ain't you, daddy?
FATHER:	You can say that again!
BRICE:	You're really sick, ain't you, daddy?
FATHER:	I heard you the first time! And I'll be still sicker if I don't get it straightened out.
BRICE:	Shall I call the doctor?
FATHER:	I don't need the doctor. All I want is a little co-operation from you!
BRICE:	Me?
FATHER:	Yes!
BRICE:	What side shall I operate on?

FATHER:	On the outside! Snooks, haven't you got any homework to do?
BRICE:	Uh-huh.
FATHER:	Well, go and do it.
BRICE:	I don't like to do it.
FATHER:	Well - pretend you like it.
BRICE:	No - I'll pretend I done it.
FATHER:	I don't care what you do! All I want is privacy. Leave my presence.
BRICE:	I ain't got presents, daddy.
FATHER:	Oh, stop it! Now, let me have a look at these expend-
BRICE:	I didn't even know it was your birthday.
FATHER:	It's not my birthday!
BRICE:	Then who gave you presents?
FATHER:	Nobody!
BRICE:	Ohhh!
FATER:	Snooks - you simply must leave this room!
BRICE:	Why?
FATHER:	Number one - I must balance these books! Number two - my boss is coming here! Number three - you're going to do your homework!
BRICE:	Number four, you're gonna help me with it.
FATHER:	Number five, I am not! Number six seven eight nine ten you're getting out of here!

BRICE:	Number twelve fourteen ninety-six - no I ain't!
FATHER:	What's going on here?
BRICE:	Let's play some more, daddy.
FATHER:	I'm not playing! You don't seem to understand, Snooks - there are times when a man simply must work.
BRICE:	Why?
FATHER:	Because I've got a wife and two children!
BRICE:	Why?
FATHER:	So you're beginning to wonder, too! I've been asking myself that question for nine years!
BRICE:	What's the answer?
FATHER:	If I knew I wouldn't have to work for a living.
BRICE:	You're dumb, ain't you, daddy?
FATHER:	That's none of your business! I made my bed and now I'll lie in it. And it's got nothing to do with beds or lying - does that answer your question?
BRICE:	I didn't ask you nothing.
FATHER:	Well, don't! I don't want any interruptions for the next fifteen minutes, understand?
BRICE:	Understand.
FATHER:	Now, where's my petty cash journal? Here. Hmmm.
BRICE:	What's in it, daddy?
FATHER:	Records of trivial expenditures. Like postage stamps - paper clips - ink -

BRICE: And your salary.

FATHER: Yes - No! Go and do your homework!

BRICE: You help me with it.

FATHER: I will not! If I keep on doing your homework you'll just wind up a big dunce!

BRICE: That's what my teacher said.

FATHER: Certainly! I did your whole arithmetic lesson for you last week, didn't I?

BRICE: Uh-huh.

FATHER: Well, what did it get you?

BRICE: A zero.

FATHER: What do you mean?

BRICE: Remember I asked you how much was a million dollars?

FATHER: Yes, I remember.

BRICE: Well, a heck of a lot ain't the right answer.

FATHER: It's still the right answer as far as I'm concerned. If I had it I could tell my boss what to do with his broken down job!

BRICE: What?

FATHER: Never mind. I'm still three thousand dollars short and you're not helping me find my error.

BRICE: Well, you ain't helping me with my homework.

FATHER: I can't help you now! I'm in a terrific jam!

BRICE:	I want some jam.
FATHER:	Oh, what's the use? What's your homework - I'll rip it out for you in ten seconds.
BRICE:	It's geography.
FATHER:	Okay, okay. Hurry up - give me the questions! Get a pencil.
BRICE:	Awight. I ain't got no paper.
FATHER:	Take any paper! First question. What is the equator? Answer, the equator is an imaginary line that runs around the earth.
BRICE:	Who let him out?
FATHER:	Who let who out?
BRICE:	The menagerie lion.
FATHER:	I didn't say menagerie lion! I said imaginary line! It means non-existent – nothing. Put it down.
BRICE:	Put nothing down?
FATHER:	No - the answer!
BRICE:	Well, what's the answer?
FATHER:	I just told you! The equator is an imaginary line running around the earth, everywhere equally distant from the two poles, and dividing the earth's surface into two hemispheres. Got it?
BRICE:	Uh-huh.
FATHER:	Are you sure?

BRICE:	Uh-huh.
FATHER:	What did I say?
BRICE:	I dunno.
FATHER:	I thought so. Second question. If you were to drill a hole thru the center of the globe where would you come out?
BRICE:	Answer. Out of the hole.
FATHER:	No - they want to know which country. What's the shape of the earth?
BRICE:	Round.
FATHER:	How do you know it's round?
BRICE:	All right - it's flat. I don't wanna argue.
FATHER:	It is round! Look - here's a globe. I start to dig a hole here at the top. Where do I come out?
BRICE:	At the bottom.
FATHER:	I know at the bottom! But which country? Suppose we start in America. Now - dig a hole!
BRICE:	Awight.
	(RIP)
FATHER:	Why did you stick your pencil into the globe?
BRICE:	I dug a hole.
FATHER:	I didn't want you to dig into this globe!
BRICE:	Why?
FATHER:	Oh, never mind! You start digging in America - you come out in Australia – I think. Put that down.

BRICE:	Awight.
FATHER:	Hmmm - I must be right because the next question is about Australia. Australia produces more sheep than any country in the world. Name the members of the sheep family.
BRICE:	Er - Charlie, Tommy, Louie -
FATHER:	No! What's the father sheep called?
BRICE:	Daddy.
FATHER:	It's called a ram. The mother sheep is ewe.
BRICE:	Me?
FATHER:	Not me - ewe!
BRICE:	Is you the mummy sheep?
FATHER:	Yes. Ewe is the mummy sheep!
BRICE:	I thought you was.
FATHER:	Ewe is!
BRICE:	I thought you *is*.
FATHER:	Well, nobody's arguing with you! The daddy sheep is called a ram, the mummy sheep is ewe, and the baby sheep is a lamb. Put it down.
BRICE:	I got it.
FATHER:	What have you got?
BRICE:	You're the mummy, ram the daddy, and lamb the baby!
FATHER:	Okay. The rest of the questions are simple - take them and let me finish my work.

BRICE:	Awight, daddy.
FATHER:	Wait a minute - where are you going with my books?
BRICE:	To finish my homework.
FATHER:	But I need those books - I have to show them to my boss.
BRICE:	I gotta show them to my teacher.
FATHER:	What on earth for?
BRICE:	I done my homework in them.
FATHER:	You what?
BRICE:	(LAUGHS) Ain't I smart?
FATHER:	You little - (SLAP)
BRICE:	Waaaahhhhh!

(MUSIC.....APPLAUSE)

MAXWELL HOUSE 2/15/40 (REVISED)

BRICE:	(SINGS) Oh, Johnny, Oh Johnny how you can love - Oh, Johnny -
FATHER:	Snooks! Quiet!
BRICE:	I wanna sing, daddy.
FATHER:	You've asked to sing every week for the last six weeks!
BRICE:	Seven.
FATHER:	I don't care if it's forty! You can't sing on this program.
BRICE:	Why?

FATHER:	Because you don't sing well enough.
BRICE:	Why?
FATHER:	Your voice hasn't developed yet! It'll get better as you grow older.
BRICE:	Ohh...daddy?
FATHER:	Yes?
BRICE:	When is my birthday?
FATHER:	Oh, it's not far off. Why do you ask?
BRICE:	I wanna know when I have to start being good!
FATHER:	That's a fine thing! You should always be good.
BRICE:	Why?
FATHER:	Because nobody likes naughty girls. People like to see children well-reared.
BRICE:	Ain't I well-reared, daddy?
FATHER:	Yes - but sometimes you misbehave terribly.
MEREDITH:	I'll say she does! She needs plenty disciplining!
BRICE:	He's here again, daddy.
FATHER:	Listen, Meredith, since when do I need your help in raising my child?
MEREDITH:	Boy, you sure need somebody's help!
BRICE:	I didn't do nothin'!
MEREDITH:	There she goes with that bad grammar again!
FATHER:	There's nothing wrong with her grammar!

BRICE:	There's nothing wrong with my grandpa either!
FATHER:	You keep quiet! What are you hinting at, Meredith?
MEREDITH:	Well, she said, "I didn't do nothin.'"
FATHER:	Well?
BRICE:	Well?
MEREDITH:	Well - where's your "G", young lady?
BRICE:	Gee - I didn't do nothin'!
FATHER:	That's better. Satisfied, professor?
MEREDITH:	No! How is she in arithmetic?
FATHER:	She's as good as you are - ask her anything!
MEREDITH:	Okay. Snooks - here's a problem. Suppose I lay two eggs on the table – and I lay two eggs on the piano - and I lay three eggs on the floor -
BRICE:	(LAUGHS)
MEREDITH:	What are you laughing at?
BRICE:	I don't believe you can do it!
FATHER:	Oh, come on! I'll school you at home!
BRICE:	(LAUGHS) Goodbye, Mr. Willson!
MEREDITH:	The child is an illiterate if I ever seen one!
	(MUSIC)
	(APPLAUSE)

The Newspaper
(March 7, 1940)

MAXWELL HOUSE
3/7/40

BRICE:	Daddy.
FATHER:	Snooks, I'm reading the paper and I'd appreciate it very much if you don't disturb me.
BRICE:	Why?
FATHER:	Because I want to relax! Do you mind if I ask you to leave the room?
BRICE:	I don't mind.
FATHER:	That's fine......Well, I don't see you leaving!
BRICE:	You know why, daddy?
FATHER:	Why?
BRICE:	'Cause I'm staying.
FATHER:	Oh, Snooks - what is it you want?
SNOOKS:	Read me the funnies.
FATHER:	No! I want read the market reports.
BRICE:	Then read me the market reports.

FATHER:	Here's a piece of a paper. Go and read it yourself.
BRICE:	Awight..... (READS SLOWLY) Ham and Eggs revived in council -
FATHER:	Snooks! Can't you read to yourself?
BRICE:	I am, daddy.
FATHER:	I mean without talking!
BRICE:	Can you read without talking?
FATHER:	Certainly.
BRICE:	Let me hear you.
FATHER:	If I don't talk how can you hear me?
BRICE:	Well, if I don't hear you how do I know you're reading?
FATHER:	You don't have to know it! I know it!
BRICE:	Why?
FATHER:	Oh, leave me alone! And don't read out loud - understand!
BRICE:	Understand... (READS SLOWLY) Do you know this woman's buttonhook?
FATHER:	What's that?
BRICE:	Here's a picture of a lady - and it says do you know this woman's buttonhook?
FATHER:	Let me see it....It says "Do you know this woman!" Where'd you get that buttonhook?
BRICE:	Right there.

FATHER: That's a question mark! Buttonhook!

BRICE: Buttonhook!

FATHER: That woman was found wandering around the streets. She's an aphasia victim. Hmmmm...Very interesting.

BRICE: What is it, daddy?

FATHER: The poor lady doesn't know who she is - and she can't remember anything. She's suffering from verbal amnesia.

BRICE: I want some, daddy.

FATHER: Some what?

BRICE: Milk of magnesia.

BRICE: I said verbal amnesia. It's a mental disorder in which the afflicted person displays an inability to remember the proper words.

BRICE: Bad, ain't it?

FATHER: Very bad. For instance, if you hold this newspaper up to an amnesiac and asked him to name it, he might call it a bottle.

BRICE: Why?

FATHER: Because there's a disturbance of perception, probably caused by hysteria or psychic trauma which irritates the lenticular zone, I think.

BRICE: (LAUGHS)

FATHER: What are you laughing at?

BRCE: I dunno.

FATHER:	It's a very serious condition. When it happens the patient usually forgets everything that occurred up to the moment of the shock.
BRICE:	I wanna catch it, daddy.
FATHER:	What for?
BRICE:	Then I won't have to do homework.
FATHER:	Never mind that! You go and do your homework this very minute – otherwise you'll catch something else.
BRICE:	Awight. Goodbye, daddy.
FATHER:	Hmm I don't like it - she's too darned obedient. Oh, well, at least I can read in peace now.
	(MUSIC.....APPLAUSE)
POWELL:	And now, ladies and gentlemen, here is Fanny Brice as Baby Snooks!
	(MUSIC.....APPLAUSE)
POWELL:	Trouble has already developed. Daddy, played by Hanley Stafford, let Snooks out of his sight for a few minutes and she disappeared. After hours of frantic telephoning he's finally discovered her in a police station – and she claims she doesn't know who she is! Listen......
COP:	Yes sir, we got a kid here all right - but she don't know her name.
FATHER:	I'm sure it's my child. The description is perfect. Can I see her?
COP:	The doctor's in there with her now. Boy, she's a holy terror!

FATHER: That's Snooks, all right. What has she done?

COP: What ain't she done! Grabbed the keys from the jailer and turned all the prisoners loose.

FATHER: Ohhh!

COP: And after we give her around five pounds of candy, too. She eats like a crocodile!

FATHER: Don't tell me. Let me see her - quick.

COP: Say - are you sure you're her old man?

FATHER: Of course I am!

COP: You're in your right mind, ain't you?

FATHER: Certainly!

COP: Beats me, brother.

FATHER: What are you talking about?

COP: If that's your kid - I can't see any reason why you come down to claim her.

FATHER: Listen, officer - I made my bed and now I gotta lie in it! Take me to her.

(DOOR OPENS AND CLOSES)

COP: Here's the doc, now. Better talk to him.

FATHER: Hello, doctor - I'm Mr. Higgins - the little girl's father. Is she all right?

DOC: Yes, she's fine, Mr. Higgins - but I'm afraid she's suffering from an attack of amnesia.

FATHER: She's faking, doctor. I know she is.

DOC:	Why do you say that?
FATHER:	Because I know where she got the idea. I read an item to her today about a woman with amnesia.
DOC:	Mr. Higgins - are you questioning my diagnosis?
FATHER:	No, doctor - but I -
DOC:	It's a true case of amnesia if I ever saw one - and I've seen plenty. Come in with me.

(DOOR OPENS AND CLOSES)

FATHER:	Snooks! Oh, Snooks!
BRICE:	Hello.
FATHER:	You see, doctor! She knows me!
DOC:	Don't be too sure. Er - do you know who this is, little girl?
BRICE:	Uh-huh.
FATHER:	There, wiseguy! What did I tell you! Tell him who I am, Snooks.
BRICE:	Seabiscuit.
FATHER:	What!
DOC:	Well, Mr. Higgins?
FATHER:	I don't understand it! She must know - it can't be possible.
DOC:	(SMUGLY) Oh, yes it can!
BRICE:	Oh, yes it can!

DOC:	The child doesn't even know her own name.
FATHER:	She does, too! It's Snooks.
BRICE:	No, it ain't.
FATHER:	Well, what is it?
BRICE:	Stinky.
FATHER:	I swear she's putting it on. Isn't there any test you can give her?
DOC:	If you'll just remain quiet for a few moments, I'll give her a test to determine her retentive powers.
FATHER:	Okay, doctor.
BRICE:	I'm hungry.
FATHER:	I'll take you home soon, Snooks - then we can have -
DOC:	Please!
FATHER:	Excuse me.
DOC:	Be good enough to hand me that telephone.
FATHER:	Certainly. Here, doctor.
DOC:	Snooks - you see what I have in my hand?
BRICE:	Uh-huh?
DOC:	Good. Now, I'm going to call off a list of words and when I come to the correct name, you stop me.
FATHER:	(WHISPERS) It's a telephone, Snooks.
DOC:	Please! Mr. Higgins, there will be no prompting.
FATHER:	Excuse me, doc.

DOC:	Ready, Snooks?
BRICE:	Ready, doc.
DOC:	Hmmm. Is this a pencil?
BRICE:	No.
DOC:	Is it a watch?
BRICE:	No.
FATHER:	Is it a telephone?
BRICE:	(YELLS) Please!
FATHER:	Excuse me. Huh?
DOC:	Mr. Higgins, if you persist in interfering I shall have to leave the room.
FATHER:	It won't happen again, doctor.
DOC:	Thank you. We'll proceed. Snooks, look at this object again. Is it a steering wheel?
BRICE:	No, it ain't.
DOC:	You're sure it's none of those things I mentioned?
BRICE:	I'm sure.
DOC:	Fine. Can you name it?
BRICE:	Uh-huh.
FATHER:	(BREATHES) Thank Heaven.
DOC:	What is it?
BRICE:	It's a diaper.

FATHER:	Ohhh! Snooks - what's the matter with you? It's a telephone!
DOC:	Are you sure, Mr. Higgins?
FATHER:	Of course I'm - it is a telephone, isn't it?
DOC:	Is there any doubt in your mind?
FATHER:	I don't know - I'm not sure. What's going on here?
BRICE:	The man is crazy, doctor.
DOC:	Snooks - this object is a telephone. It happens to be a telephone extension - have you any idea what an extension is used for?
BRICE:	Uh-huh.
DOC:	What?
BRICE:	So Mummy can listen in on Daddy.
FATHER:	Aha! You see - she does know who she is! She just gave herself away.
DOC:	Mr. Higgins, you're making it very difficult for me to conduct this examination. The child has shown no signs of returning to a normal state. The fact that she mentioned a mummy and a daddy proves absolutely nothing!
BRICE:	So there, wiseguy!
FATHER:	She's faking this so she won't have to go to school!
BRICE:	No, I ain't.
FATHER:	Then why are you doing it?

BRICE: 'Cause I want some more candy!

FATHER: Then you admit your faking! I knew it all -

DOC: Stop this! Snooks -

BRICE: That ain't my name. I don't know who I am.

FATHER: You do, too!

BRICE: Waaaaaahhhh! I think I'm a married woman and I got six children.

FATHER: Ahhhh - nonsense. Let me take her home, Doc. I'll refresh her memory.

DOC: Mr. Higgins - you're only aggravating the condition. I know how to discover whether or not she's malingering, if you'll only let me!

BRICE: Yeah.

FATHER: Forgive me, doctor. I'm terribly upset.

DOC: Very well. We'll continue with the telephone experiment. Snooks, I want you to call a number on this telephone.

BRICE: Which number?

DOC: I want you to try and remember this number - Oxford 5580.

FATHER: Oxford 5580. That's an easy number, Snooks. Just think of -

DOC: Mr. Higgins! .... Can you remember it, Snooks?

BRICE: No.

DOC:	Well, here's a very simple way to do it. Oxford - think of an ox or a cow. Five - think of your five fingers. Another five - think of your toes. Eight – think of all the candy you just ate, and oh - think of something round. Like doughnuts. Got it?
BRICE:	Got it.
DFOC:	Here's the phone. Call the number.
FATHER:	Hope she gets it right.
BRICE;	Hello... give me Cowfoot - Fingers toes candy nuts.
FATHER:	No - No! Snooks - it's Oxford five – er, five eight - er -
DOC:L	Hmmm. You see, Mr. Higgins You ever forgot it yourself.
FATHER:	That's because I'm so excited! What is the broken down number?
DOC:	It's Oxford five five – er, Oxford – er, eight five - wait a minute. I have it written down here. Oxford 5580. I'll call it.
FATHER:	I don't get the point of all this!
DOC:	You will in a minute. Hello... Get me Oxford 5580... Now take the phone, Snooks.
BRICE:	Why?
DOC:	A woman will answer it - and I want you to ask her for a lady's red hat with a mouse-colored feather on the bottom. Try and retain that.
BRICE:	Awight.... Hello.
FATHER:	A fine amnesia test!

BRICE:	Hello - I want a lady mouse bottom with a feather hat.
FATHER:	Not a lady mouse! A mouse-colored feather!
BRICE:	I want a colored mouse with a feather in the bottom.
FATHER:	No!
DOC:	Will you please let her work it out for herself. Go on, Snooks!
BRICE:	Hello. I want a lady's hat for a mouse with a red bottom!
DOC:	All right - hang up. Mr. Higgins. The child is positively suffering from amnesia.
FATHER:	Will you let me try something?
DOC:	Go ahead - try anything you like. But I'm convinced.
FATHER:	Okay. Snooks - will you try to remember who you are if I buy you a pair of skates?
BRICE:	No.
FATHER:	A new bicycle?
BRICE:	No. But I might try if you buy me a pony.
FATHER:	All right. I'll buy you a pony.
BRICE:	A brown pony?
FATHER:	Yes - a brown pony.
BRICE:	I don't like brown ponies.
FATHER:	I'll buy you any kind of pony you like if you'll remember who you are. Now, try hard.
BRICE:	I'm trying.

FATHER: Is it coming?

BRICE: It's no use, Daddy. I don't know who I am.

FATHER: Oh, I see. But you just called me Daddy, didn't you?

BRICE: Did I?

FATHER: You certainly did! Now, tell the doctor you were faking! Go on!

BRICE: Waaaahhhh! I wanna go home, daddy.

FATHER: Well, does that convince you, doctor?

DOC: She seems like she's coming out of it now. Do you feel better, Snooks?

BRICE: No, I got a headache.

DOC: When you get her home, Mr. Higgins – bathe her head in salt water.

FATHER: Bathe her head in salt water? What for?

DOC: It'll toughen the skin a little and make her insensitive to pain.

BRICE: I better sit in it, too!

FATHER: I'll say you better! Come on – we'll talk this over.

DOC: But I insist, Mr. Higgins, the child definitely had an attack. I can tell you how to avoid a recurrence, too.

FATHER: Never mind. I know how to fix her so she'll never forget.

BRICE: How?

FATHER: (SWEETLY) Snooks – I'm going to give you something that you'll remember as long as you live!

BRICE: (LAUGHS) What is it, daddy?

FATHER: Just this! (SLAP)

BRICE: WAAAAAHHHHH!

               (MUSIC….APPLAUSE)

Plane Flight
(March 14, 1940)

MAXWELL HOUSE COFFEE TIME (REVISED)

3-14-40

BRICE: Daddy!

FATHER: Snooks—I thought you were asleep. You'd better go back to bed.

BRICE: Why?

FATHER: Because it's very late.

BRICE: Where you going?

FATHER: I'm leaving tonight for Washington.

BRICE: I wanna go with you.

FATHER: Don't be ridiculous. I'm taking an airplane and there's no room for you.

BRICE: Why?

FATHER: Because I've only reserved one berth.

BRICE: What's a berth?

FATHER: It's like a bed. But on trains and planes they call them berths. I've explained this to you before.

BRICE:	Explain it again.
FATHER:	I haven't got time. Go back to bed.
BRICE:	What's a berth?
FATHER:	I told you it's a bed! They have upper berths and lower berths!
BRICE:	Which did you take?
FATHER:	An upper.
BRICE:	Why?
FATHER:	Because that's all they had.
BRICE:	It's cheaper, too.
FATHER:	Not on planes. Only on trains. Then the lower is higher than the upper.
BRICE:	Huh?
FATHER:	I mean the upper is higher, naturally—but it's lower because when you awake in a lower you don't have to get down to get up. In a lower you're already down when you're up so that's why it's higher.
BRICE:	In the lower.
FATHER:	Exactly. The berth below the one above is always the highest because it's the lowest.
BRICE:	Understand?
FATHER:	Understand. Oh, leave me alone and go back to bed.
BRICE:	I'm going with you.
FATHER:	I told you there's no room!

BRICE: I'll sleep in the middle.

FATHER: The middle?

BRICE: Yeah—because the middle is upper than the slipper and the higher is lower than blower and—

FATHER: Stop it! Snooks—please don't cause any trouble now. I don't want to miss my plane.

BRICE: Then take me with you. I'm going to Washington with you.

FATHER: Piffle! I wouldn't even consider it!

BRICE: Poffle! I'm going.

FATHER: Stop that! You've got about as much chance of going with me as—as that lamp has of jumping off the table!

(CRASH)

FATHER: Ohhh! Snooks! What did you do? [QUICK]

BRICE: It jumped off, daddy. Honest, I didn't touch it! [LAUGH]

FATHER: That's the last straw! You little—(SLAP)

BRICE: Waaaaaaahhhhh!

(MUSIC...APPLAUSE)

POWELL: Well, I can't believe that even soft-hearted Daddy would allow himself to be bullied into taking his angel child to Washington, but we'll see—we'll see. In the meantime...I'd like to give you my impression of a new tune—

"Si—Si".

"SI—SI"...POWELL & ORCHESTRA.

(APPLAUSE)

BRICE: (SINGS) We're all going to Washington! We're all going to—

FATHER: Oh, keep quiet!

BRICE: Are you mad, Daddy?

FATHER: No. I just don't understand how you wangled me into taking you along!

BRICE: I'm a good wangler, ain't I?

FATHER: You're great—stay behind that rail!

BRICE: Why?

FATHER: Because that's where the planes land. I don't want you to get hit by a flying propeller.

BRICE: Why?

FATHER: I don't know—but stay behind that rail just the same.

BRICE: Where's our plane, daddy?

FATHER: A pilot is bringing it in from San Francisco and it's not due for another five minutes.

BRICE: Maybe he got lost.

FATHER: He can't get lost. The pilot has a compass.

BRICE: What's that?

FATHER: It's an instrument—that tells you which way is north south east and west.

BRICE: Which way is it?

FATHER: You've learned the points of the compass! If you're facing north what's on your left hand?

BRICE: Fingers.

FATHER: No—it's west! And I'm not going to explain the compass to you at one o'clock in the morning!

BRICE: Why?

FATHER: Don't bother me! The pilot will bring the plane in on time.

BRICE: How will he find the way?

FATHER: He'll ask an eagle!

BRICE: What if he don't see an eagle?

FATHER: Then he'll ask a stork!

BRICE: The same stork who brings the babies?

FATHER: Yes!

BRICE: Ohhh...Daddy?

FATHER: What is it?

BRICE: Who brings the baby storks?

FATHER: I don't know. I wish that plane would hurry.

BRICE: There's a plane, daddy. Let's go on that one.

FATHER: That's a mail plane.

BRICE: How can you tell?

FATHER: By the United States Mail! They carry letters.

BRICE: I want some lettuce.

FATHER: Stop it! Watch them load the packages on that plane.

BRICE: Who's that man?

FATHER: He's the pilot. He drives the plane.

BRICE: He's been horseback riding, ain't he?

FATHER: What makes you think so?

BRICE: 'Cause he's got a pillow strapped on his—

FATHER: That's a parachute! Commercial pilots often wear them.

BRICE: Why?

FATHER: In case something happens to his plane while he's flying he can jump out. The parachute helps him land safely.

BRICE: Does he land sitting down?

FATHER: Of course not!

BRICE: Then why did he strap the pillow to his—

FATHER: I told you it's not a pillow! It's a parachute! When a pilot jumps in midair he counts three and pulls a ring. Then the parachute opens up like a big umbrella and he floats slowly down to earth.

BRICE: What if it don't open?

FATHER: He sends it back to the factory and gets a new one!

BRICE: Get me one, daddy.

FATHER: You don't need one.

BRICE: Well, how will I jump out if we have an accident?

FATHER:	Don't worry—you won't have any accidents!
BRICE:	Why?
FATHER:	Because planes today are as safe as automobiles. Safer. There are more accidents in cars than there are in planes.
BRICE:	Why?
FATHER:	Maybe it's because the pilot isn't always hugging the co-pilot.
BRICE:	Don't the pilot like the co-pilot?
FATHER:	Yes—he loves him.
BRICE:	Then why don't he hug him?
FATHER:	I don't know. I'll ask him.
BRICE:	I wanna hug a pilot.
FATHER:	I'll talk to him when we get on the plane. Shhh—I hear it coming.

(PLANE COMING IN)

BRICE:	I'm afraid to fly, daddy.
FATHER:	Now, don't start that. Come on—help daddy with the bags. Take that little one.
BRICE:	I ain't going.
FATHER:	Oh, please, Snooks! You talked me into taking you along—it's one o'clock in the morning and I simply must take the plane. I can't leave you here.
BRICE:	It's gonna fall down, daddy.
FATHER:	No it isn't—it's only landing. Look how perfect it lands!

(PLANE LANDS)

See! Come on—they're opening the door to let us on.

BRICE: Awight. Hold my hand.

FATHER: Okay. Be careful going up the gangplank—and don't make any noise.

BRICE: Who's that pretty lady, daddy?

FATHER: She's the stewardess.

BRICE: Does she hug the pilot?

FATHER: No. She'll take care of us on the trip.

BRICE: I wanna hug the pilot.

FATHER: All right—later. Let's get aboard.

STEW: (QUIETLY) Good evening. Name, please?

FATHER: Higgins. This is my child.

STEW: You're in upper and lower six. How old are you, little girl?

BRICE: I'm seven—and my daddy's thirty-five. Wanna hug him?

FATHER: Snooks! She's very tired, Miss. I'd like to get her right to bed.

STEW: Certainly. Follow me. Here we are.

BRICE: Who's in this one, Daddy?

FATHER: Stop peeking in those curtains!

BRICE: Why?

STEW: People are sleeping there, dear. Can I help you undress?

BRICE: No.

STEW:	I'll unlace your shoes.
BRICE:	I wanna get out!
FATHER:	You can't get out. We're going to take off in a second.
STEW:	That's right, dear. You'd better take off your dress.
BRICE:	Are you gonna take off, too?
STEW:	Uh-huh.
BRICE:	You take off first then I'll take off.
FATHER:	You'd better let me handle her, Miss.
STEW:	All right, sir. Call me if you need me.
FATHER:	Thank you. Come on, Snooks. Climb up that little ladder.
BRICE:	Where?
FATHER:	Right up there—in the upper. That's where you'll sleep.
BRICE:	I don't wanna sleep up there.
FATHER:	Do you want to sleep in the lower?
BRICE:	No.
FATHER:	Then where do you want to sleep?
BRICE:	With the pilot.
FATHER:	Please, Snooks—you'll wake up all the passengers in the plane. Climb up there like a good girl.
BRICE:	I'm afraid to sleep there alone.
FATHER:	Don't worry—the angels will take care of you.
BRICE:	Where's the angels, daddy?

FATHER: The plane is full of them.

MAN: (HOLLERS) Ahhh—shut up with that racket!

BRICE: Is that one of the angels, daddy?

FATHER: See! I told you to keep quiet—you woke up that man. Now, get undressed.

BRICE: Awight...daddy?

FATHER: Shhh. Yes?

BRICE: Tell me a story.

FATHER: No! Not tonight!

BRICE: Waaaaaahhhhh!

FATHER: Shhh! All right—all right!

MAN: Hey—why don't you keep that kid quiet?

FATHER: I'm awfully sorry, sir. It's her first flight and she's a little nervous. She won't disturb you anymore.

MAN: Okay.

BRICE: Tell me a story.

FATHER: All right—but a quick one. And no interruptions. Comprehend?

BRICE: Copperhead.

FATHER: (WHISPERS) This is the story of Tom Thumb.

BRICE: Ooooh—I like it.

FATHER: There was once an old couple who didn't have any children. They always wanted a little child—

BRICE:	Why?
FATHER:	Because they didn't know how well off they were. They went to a magician named Merlin and—
BRICE:	Who went?
FATHER:	The old couple. They went to him and asked him—
BRICE:	Asked who?
FATHER:	Merlin. They asked him for a child even if he was no bigger than his father's thumb. So Merlin gave them a child no bigger than his father's thumb and they called him Tom Thumb.
BRICE:	Who called him?
FATHER:	Tom's parents. They had…
BRICE:	Tom, who?
FATHER:	Tom Thumb.
BRICE:	Who's he?
FATHER:	The boy in the story.
BRICE:	Which story?
FATHER:	(YELLS) The story I'm telling you! Tom Thumb!
BRICE:	Shhhh—daddy!
FATHER:	Well, don't interrupt! As soon as Tom came to live with them the king of the fairies wanted to see him so his mother dressed him—
BRICE:	The king's mother?
FATHER:	No—Tom's mother.

BRICE:	Tom who?
MAN:	(YELLS) Tom Thumb!...Listen, mister—you'll have to put that kid to sleep or else there'll be trouble!
FATHER:	I'm sorry, she'll go to sleep now. Okay, Snooks—that's the end of the story, Goodnight.
BRICE:	Goodnight...Daddy?
FATHER:	What is it?
BRICE:	Take me down.
FATHER:	What for?
BRICE:	I want a drink!
FATHER:	All right. I'll press the button—the stewardess will bring you a drink.

(LIGHT BUZZ)

STEW:	Yes sir?
FATHER:	Will you bring a drink for my little girl, please?
STEW:	Certainly.
BRICE:	You don't have to. I don't want no drink.
FATHER:	Then why did you make me call her?
BRICE:	I wanted to make sure she wasn't hugging the pilot!

(LAUGHS)

FATHER:	Ahhhh—goodnight!
BRICE:	Ahhhh—goodnight!

(MUSIC...APPLAUSE)

POWELL:	Here it is—A bright saying of a child... acted out by Snooks and Daddy…
	Daddy's boss has been to dinner and the evening has been a great success. Then—this happened.
BOSS:	Swell dinner, Higgins.
FATHER:	Thanks, Boss. I hoped you'd like it.
BOSS:	Only one thing missing. Plums. I'm crazy about plums.
FATHER:	Well, if I'd only known—
BOSS:	Oh, never mind. I can do without them.
BRICE:	I'll go get them, daddy.
BOSS:	Well! Isn't that nice! You certainly have a model child there, Higgins.
FATHER:	Er – yes. We think so.
BRICE:	I think so, too.
FATHER:	Will you go to the store for the plums, Snooks?
PRICE:	Uh-huh.
BOSS:	Fine! Now—here's a dime. But before you buy the plums, Snooks—you'd better pinch one or two to make sure they're ripe.
BRICE:	Pinch 'em?
BOSS:	Yes.
BRICE:	Awight...Goodbye.
	(DOOR SLAM)

(MUSIC UP...FADES...DOOR OPENS)

BOSS: Oh, here's Snooks with my plums.

BRICE: I got the plums.

FATHER: That's wonderful, Snooks. And did you pinch one or two like my boss told you?

BRICE: Uh-huh.

BOSS: That's a sweet child!

BRICE: I pinched the whole bagful—and here's your dime back!

(LAUGHS)

FATHER: Ohhhhh? What's the use!

(MUSIC...APPLAUSE)

Snooks Steals a Tooth
(March 28, 1940)

MAXWELL HOUSE COFFEE TIME (REVISED)
3-28-40

POWELL: And now, ladies and gentlemen, here is Fanny Brice as Baby Snooks!

(MUSIC...APPLAUSE)

POWELL: Daddy, played by Hanley Stafford, has had a hard day at the office. He is trying to read his newspaper in the study but Snooks has been constantly running in and out. Daddy's patience is rapidly becoming exhausted. Listen...

FATHER: (MUMBLES) Kid can't sit still a minute—like trying to rest in a boiler factory!

BRICE: (OFF) London Bridge is falling down, falling down...

FATHER: Here she comes again!

BRICE: Excuse me, daddy.

FATHER: Snooks—you've been in and out of this room ten times!

BRICE: Have I?

FATHER:	Yes—and every time you come back you cross between my feet and the chair they're resting on! I don't like it!
BRICE:	Why?
FATHER:	Because I don't like having to take my feet off!
BRICE:	Can you take your feet off, daddy?
FATHER:	I mean off the chair! Why don't you walk around me?
BRICE:	It's too easy!
FATHER:	I thought so. Well, I'm warning you—don't disturb me anymore! Understand?
BRICE:	Understand. (SINGS) London Bridge is falling down, falling—
FATHER:	Stop that singing!
BRICE:	Awight...Daddy?
FATHER:	What is it?
BRICE:	Who's London?
FATHER:	London is the name of a city.
BRICE:	Ain't it a man?
FATHER:	No!
BRICE:	Then why is his britches falling down?
FATHER:	It's not britches—it's bridge! London Bridge!
	(BABY CRIES FROM OFF)
FATHER:	Did you hear something?
	(BABY CRIES)

BRICE:	It's that kid of yours.
FATHER:	Robespierre! He's crying – I'll see what it is.
	(BABY YELLS)
BRICE:	(IMITATES HIM) Waaaaahhh. All he does is holler!
FATHER:	(FROM OFF) Snooks! What do you think?
BRICE:	What?
FATHER:	(VERY HAPPY) You can't imagine what's happened to little Robespierre!
BRICE:	His nose dropped off.
FATHER:	No—he's got a tooth! His first tooth! Come and have a look at him.
BRICE:	Who?
FATHER:	Your little brother.
BRICE:	I ain't got no little brother.
FATHER:	You haven't got a little brother?
BRICE:	No—I divorced him.
FATHER:	I never heard of such nonsense! Snooks, I can't understand why you don't show any affection at all for Robespierre.
BRICE:	I don't like him.
FATHER:	Why not?
BRICE:	He hollers too much.
FATHER:	Of course he cries a lot. But that's only his way of letting us know he wants something.

BRICE: Well, why don't he ask for it?

FATHER: Snooks, you know as well as I do that infants can't talk!

BRICE: Why?

FATHER: Because nobody talks until he's at least a year old.

BRICE: That ain't what you said to Uncle Louie.

FATHER: What did I say to Uncle Louie?

BRICE: You said you cursed the day you was born.

FATHER: That has nothing to do with it! Come and have a look at your brother's new tooth.

BRICE: No—pull it out and bring it here.

FATHER: You little savage! You'll be sorry for treating your brother like this.

BRICE: Why?

(BABY HOLLERS)

FATHER: He's crying—I'm going in there. Are you coming?

BRICE: Awight—but I'll only take a quick look.

FATHER: Don't make too much noise... He's still half asleep...

(BABY WHIMPERS QUIETLY THEN STOPS)

BRICE: He stopped, daddy.

FATHER: Yes. Shhh...Look at that little angel...What a beautiful complexion.

BRICE: He looks like a lobster.

FATHER: Well—he is a little red.

BRICE: Is only babies faces red?

FATHER: Oh, no. Sometimes grown people's faces get red.

BRICE: Why?

FATHER: Oh, for various reasons. Mostly a person's face turns red when he's ashamed.

BRICE: Ohhh...Daddy?

FATHER: Yes?

BRICE: Why does Uncle Louie only get ashamed in his nose?

FATHER: We won't discuss that now.

BRICE: Why?

FATHER: Shhhh...Maybe Robespierre will open his mouth and then you can see his tooth.

BRICE: Stick a pin in him.

FATHER: I should say not! How can you think of hurting that little mite. He's so sweet—and innocent. Snooks—take a good look at him. You may be looking at a future president. (TENDERLY) I wonder what the fates have in store for him...Maybe he'll be a famous artist—or a physician...I know he's going to make us all proud...You'll be happy to point him out as your brother...Look at that firm little chin—that well-shaped head. What a child!... Snooks—you're thinking, aren't you?

BRICE: Yes, daddy.

FATHER: I thought so. What are you thinking about?

BRICE: How long is a snake's tail?

FATHER:	Ahh—you haven't got an ounce of sentiment in your body!
	(BABY CRIES SOFTLY)
BRICE:	He's bawling again.
FATHER:	Look – look! Right there in front—see the tooth? Isn't it wonderful?
BRICE:	What's wonderful about it?
FATHER:	Well—it's his first tooth!
BRICE:	Can he take it out?
FATHER:	Of course not! Nobody takes their teeth out!
BRICE:	You always take—
FATHER:	Never mind that! My teeth have nothing to do with you.
BRICE:	Why do you put them in a glass of—
FATHER:	Snooks! I'll thank you not to bandy my teeth about! I'm not as young as I used to be and those things happen!
BRICE:	Why?
FATHER:	Let me explain something to you. To begin with – whether you like it or not, in a very short time all of your teeth will fall out!
BRICE:	I like it.
FATHER:	Oh, you do, eh?
BRICE:	Uh-huh. I'll stick 'em in a pumpkin for Hallowe'en.
FATHER:	Very funny. All I'm trying to tell you is that your mouth is full of deciduous teeth.

BRICE:	I don't taste nothing.
FATHER:	Of course not. It just means you'll lose them—they're milk teeth.
BRICE:	Can I milk 'em?
FATHER:	No! And remember, when a tooth falls out, put it under your pillow.
BRICE:	What for?
FATHER:	Well—a Brownie will come while you're asleep and turn the tooth into a dime.
BRICE:	I wanna pull one out now.
FATHER:	Don't be silly. I'm just trying to impress on your mind that teeth are vitally important to your health. You know how many types of teeth there are?
BRICE:	No.
FATHER:	Well, there's the incisors, the canines, the bicuspids, the molars—and later on you'll get wisdom teeth.
BRICE:	Wisdom teeth?
FATHER:	Yes.
BRICE:	When did you get them?
FATHER:	Mine came very late. As a matter of fact I didn't get my wisdom teeth until after I was married.
BRICE:	Too late, huh?
FATHER:	It's not necessary to make those remarks! (Darn kid's uncanny!)

BRICE: Huh?

FATHER: Nothing. And don't try to loosen your teeth!

BRICE: I wanna pull one out.

FATHER: What for?

BRICE: I want the Brownie to change it into a dime.

FATHER: Your teeth are still too tight. You'll have to be patient.

BRICE: Oh...Is Robespierre's tooth loser than mine?

FATHER: I suppose so. Let's go back to the study.

BRICE: You go, Daddy...I wanna stay here a little while.

(PAUSE)

FATHER: Snooks—what have you got in your mind?

BRICE: Nothing.

FATHER: Are you thinking of tampering with the baby's tooth?

BRICE: Who, me?

FATHER: Don't put on that innocent face! Were you actually going to—to—Oh, I can't say it!

BRICE: I can say it, daddy. Pull the baby's tooth?

FATHER: (AGHAST) Snooks—you weren't!

BRICE: He don't need it—he don't eat meat.

FATHER: Young lady—step outside with me.

(DOOR OPENS AND CLOSES)

FATHER: You realize the terrible thoughts you've been harboring?

BRICE:	Uh-huh.
FATHER:	Is there anything you'd care to say in your defense?
BRICE:	No. Shall I turn over?
FATHER:	There's no alternative.
BRICE:	Ain't it awful?
FATHER:	(SIGHS) Here we go again. (SLAP)
BRICE:	WAAAAAAAHHHHHH!
	(MUSIC...APPLAUSE)
	(CLOCK CHIMES THREE TIMES)
DADDY:	(SNORES)
BRICE:	Daddy!
FATHER:	Huh? What is it? Snooks!
BRICE:	I think there's a burglar downstairs.
FATHER:	What makes you think so?
BRICE:	'Cause I heard a noise.
FATHER:	Burglars don't make noise.
BRICE:	Why?
FATHER:	Because they'd get caught all the time. If you heard a noise you can be sure it wasn't a burglar.
BRICE:	Do you hear any noise now?
FATHER:	No. No—I don't hear a sound.
PRICE:	Then there must be a burglar down there.

FATHER: Why do you say that?

BRICE: 'Cause he ain't making any noise.

FATHER: Oh, bosh! Go to sleep.

BRICE: Oh, bosh! I'm scared.

FATHER: Listen, Snooks—you just woke up scared because you probably had a nightmare.

BRICE: What's that?

FATHER: A bad dream.

BRICE: No, daddy. I had a beautiful dream.

FATHER: That's fine.

BRICE: Shall I tell you about it?

FATHER: No—tell me in the morning.

BRICE: I wanna tell you now!

FATHER: All right—tell me now. Hurry up.

BRICE: Well—I dreamed I went to Heaven.

FATHER: A likely story!

BRICE: Huh?

FATHER: Nothing. Go on with your dream.

BRICE: And I flew over the chimneys and on top of the clouds until I came to some big gates.

FATHER: Make it short!

BRICE: Awight. Then I met an angel with a long beard and golden wings.

FATHER:	Yes.
BRICE:	No—I think he had long wings and a golden beard.
FATHER:	What's the difference—finish your dream.
BRICE:	He gave me a piece of chalk.
FATHER:	What for?
BRICE:	He showed me a big ladder—and I had to climb up it and make a chalk mark for every wicked thing I ever done.
FATHER:	Hmm—go on.
BRICE:	I was standing on the first step of the ladder trying to think of some wicked things—
FATHER:	That's a tough job for you. Continue.
BRICE:	When I saw you coming down!
FATHER:	Me?
BRICE:	Uh-huh. You was coming down the ladder!
FATHER:	What for?
BRICE:	More chalk! (LAUGHS)
FATHER:	Ahhh—goodnight!
BRICE:	Ahhh—goodnight!
	(MUSIC...APPLAUSE)

The Phone Bill
(April 4, 1940)

MAXWELL HOUSE COFFEE TIME

April 4, 1940

POWELL: And now, ladies and gentlemen, here is Fanny Brice as Baby Snooks!

(MUSIC...APPLAUSE)

POWELL: Daddy, played by Hanley Stafford, has received an enormous bill from the telephone company including a charge of twelve dollars for a long-distance call which completely mystifies him. As the scene opens we find him on the phone talking to the company's business manager. Listen...

FATHER: Well, look here—er—what did you say your name was?

MAN: (FILTER) Barley I. P. Barley

FATHER: Yes. Well, Mr. Barley, I'm quite sure there's been a mistake about this call for twelve dollars. Neither I nor my wife made any long-distance calls this month.

MAN: (FILTER) I see. Mr. Higgins, I'd like to check this with the charge operator. Do you mind if I call you back?

FATHER: Okay. Goodbye.

MAN:	Thank you—goodbye. (HANGS UP)
FATHER:	Broken-down phone company! Plenty nerve putting a charge like that on my bill! Hmmm!
	(DOOR OPENS AND CLOSES)
BRICE:	Hello, Daddy.
FATHER:	Hello, Snooks. Did you mail my letter?
BRICE:	Uh-huh. Here's your two cents back.
FATHER:	I told you to buy a stamp with that money.
BRICE:	I didn't need no stamp.
FATHER:	What do you mean?
BRICE:	I sneaked the letter in the box when nobody was looking.
FATHER:	That's a fine thing! That's wonderful! [Oh Snooks]
BRICE:	You like it, daddy? [No good?]
FATHER:	No, I don't like it! [Of course not!] I don't want people to think I'm a cheapskate for a measly two cents!
BRICE:	Why?
FATHER:	Because I'm not a cheapskate!
BRICE:	Ain't you?
FATHER:	No.
BRICE:	Then give me the two cents.
FATHER:	Oh, all right. You've been a pretty good girl today.
BRICE:	I couldn't help being good.

FATHER:	Why not?
BRICE:	I got a stiff neck.
FATHER:	I see. I thought it wasn't natural. [Now] Anyway, run along and let me—
	(PHONE RINGS)
FATHER:	Hello.
MAN:	(FILTER) Mr. Higgins, this is Mr. Barley again.
FATHER:	Oh, yes.
MAN:	I'm sorry, but that call was made from your house on April first. It was a party to party call to New York.
FATHER:	New York!
MAN:	That's right. I've talked to the operator who handled the call and she says it sounded like a child.
FATHER:	(OMINOUSLY) Uh-huh! A child!
BRICE:	Oh-oh.
MAN:	The party called was a Mr. Louie—
FATHER:	Never mind! Thanks a lot – goodbye! (SLAMS RECEIVER)
BRICE:	I think I'll go out and play.
FATHER:	Stay here, you! Snooks!
BRICE:	Yes, daddy?
FATHER:	Why are you running out in such a hurry?
BRICE:	I thought you said goodbye to me.

FATHER:	(DELIBERATELY) I said goodbye to the manager of the telephone company.
BRICE:	Oh...Is he going someplace?
FATHER:	No. He has a dreary job that keeps him in his office all the time.
BRICE:	Why?
FATHER:	He has to check long-distance telephone calls.
BRICE:	Oh. Dreary, ain't it?
FATHER:	Very! Er—Snooks. Have you any idea how much a call to New York costs?
BRICE:	No.
FATHER:	Of course, you wouldn't dream of making a telephone call to New York.
BRICE:	Wouldn't I?
FATHER:	I don't think so. Would you?
BRICE:	Would it make somebody mad?
FATHER:	It certainly would.
BRICE:	I wouldn't dream of it, daddy.
FATHER:	That's what I thought. Snooks! Look at me!
BRICE:	Awight... (LAUGHS)...Waaaahhhh!
FATHER:	What are you yelling about?
BRICE:	You got that spank look on your face.
FATHER:	That's strange. You haven't done anything that I should

	spank you, have you?
BRICE:	I didn't call up Uncle Louie!
FATHER:	I didn't say you did!
BRICE:	But you're gonna say it.
FATHER:	What makes you think so?
BRICE:	Huh?
FATHER:	If you have no guilty knowledge, what prompted you to remark that you didn't call up Uncle Louie?
BRICE:	I said the wrong thing, huh?
FATHER:	It would appear so. As a matter of fact—somebody did call Uncle Louie in New York and the telephone company has charged me for the call. Now—who did it?
BRICE:	Er—could it be the cook?
FATHER:	No—it couldn't be the cook!
BRICE:	Why?
FATHER:	Because that was her day off.
BRICE:	It couldn't be the cook.
FATHER:	No, and it couldn't have been mother because she was staying at Grandma's.
BRICE:	How about—
FATHER:	Robespierre can't even talk—if that's what you're thinking.
BRICE:	That's what I was thinking.

FATHER: And I know *I* didn't make the call—so it leaves only one person in this household!

BRICE: The boarder.

FATHER: We haven't got any boarders!

BRICE: Ohhh! Let's take in some boarders, daddy.

FATHER: Snooks! I've eliminated everybody except you.

BRICE: Can't I have some, too?

FATHER: Some what?

BRICE: Some lemonade.

FATHER: I said eliminated—not lemonade! Now, in the face of this overwhelming evidence could it be possible that you'll deny you made the call? Could that be?

BRICE: Could be.

FATHER: Very well. Then I'll tell you this. I just had the call checked and the charge operator said it was made by a little girl.

BRICE: All right—I'll give you the nickel.

FATHER: Nickel! That call cost twelve dollars!

BRICE: (QUICKLY) I didn't do it!

FATHER: Oh, you didn't, eh? But you were just willing to pay a nickel for it!

BRICE: I figure it's cheaper than arguing. [A woman's got a night to change your mind, ain't she?]

FATHER:	Snooks, I'm warning you! You'd better make a clean breast of this whole thing! I must have the truth and from your own lips!...Now – start talking! [Now – tell me everything!]
BRICE:	Awight...Er – Did you know our pussy-cat had six kittens today?
FATHER:	What about it?
BRICE:	I didn't even know she was married.
FATHER:	That's entirely irrelevant!
BRICE:	Yeah why don't she bring her husband around?
FATHER:	Stop it! Now, Snooks – I want a full confession! I want the truth!
BRICE:	Awight, daddy.
FATHER:	Who made the call?
BRICE:	The cat done it.
FATHER:	The cat!
BRICE:	She wanted to tell her husband that she had six kitt—
FATHER:	I told you I want the truth! Why did you make that call?
BRICE:	I didn't wanna do it—but they made me!
FATHER:	Who made you?
BRICE:	The four Indians!
FATHER:	What four Indians?
BRICE:	What did you say, daddy?

FATHER:	You said four Indians made you call Uncle Louie. (OMINOUSLY) Well—is that all?
BRICE:	Ain't it enough?
FATHER:	Not quite! I refuse to believe any story about Indians!
BRICE:	Will you believe it about cowboys?
FATHER:	No!
BRICE:	G-Men?
FATHER:	I won't listen to any of that ridiculous nonsense! You made a call to New York that cost twelve dollars! Why did you do it—and remember I want the truth!
BRICE:	Awight.
FATHER:	Well?
BRICE:	A dragon walked in so I got scared and called Uncle Louie.
FATHER:	Oh, a dragon, eh?
BRICE:	Uh-huh. [Yeah.]
FATHER:	I see. And what did this dragon walk in for?
BRICE:	I think he was a census taker.
FATHER:	All right, Snooks—I've had enough of this!
BRICE:	Me too—goodbye!
FATHER:	Stay here! I've listened to your fantastic stories long enough—and now I want the truth! Comprehend?
BRICE:	Copperhead.

FATHER:	I want you to tell me exactly what happened when you called Uncle Louie in New York. Go ahead.
BRICE:	Awight. I found his number in your little black book.
FATHER:	My little black book?
BRICE:	I found some other numbers there, too.
FATHER:	Never mind that!
BRICE:	Who's Fifi, daddy?
FATHER:	You little snoop—go on with your story!
BRICE:	Well, I called the number and then I waited—
FATHER:	Yes?
BRICE:	Then Uncle Louie said hello.
FATHER:	Go on!
BRICE:	Then I said hello and he said who is this?
FATHER:	Continue.
BRICE:	Then I said, "This is the Pot O'Gold program. You win a thousand dollars."
FATHER:	Good heavens. What did he do?
BRICE:	I think he fainted.
FATHER:	I see! Then what happened?
BRICE:	I waited a few minutes to see if he was alive—
FATHER:	Yes?
BRICE:	Then I said "April Fool"—and hung up.

FATHER:	And he never knew it was you?
BRICE:	No.
FATHER:	I wish I could have seen his face! (STARTS TO LAUGH) I bet he's still waiting for the money. (LAUGHS)
BRICE:	Ain't you gonna spank me?
FATHER:	No. It's worth twelve dollars to see that tightwad get it in the neck! Here's a dime—go out and play!
BRICE:	Do you feel all right, daddy?
FATHER:	I never felt better in my life! (DIES LAUGHING)
BRICE:	(LAUGHS TOO) Goodbye, daddy!
	(MUSIC...APPLAUSE)
POWELL:	Bravo, Mary! That was a real treat! Now we continue with—
STAFFORD:	Excuse me, Dick.
POWELL:	Oh, hello, daddy.
STAFFORD:	Did I hear you say you bagged some wild boar?
POWELL:	Er—no. I didn't say I bagged any. But I did go hunting for them.
MERE:	(YELLS) Hey, Mary! Come back here—he's gonna tell about it.
MARTIN:	Oh, I don't wanna miss this.
POWELL:	What's all the excitement about?
BRICE:	Yeah. What's all the excitement about?

POWELL:	Oh, Snooks! Don't sneak up on me like that!
BRICE:	Why?
STAFFORD:	Keep still, Snooks. Where did you go hunting, Dick?
POWELL:	Catalina. Joan and I go almost every week-end.
BRICE:	Who's Joan, daddy?
STAFFORD:	Shh—that's Joan Blondell, Mrs. Powell.
BRICE:	Oh. Is it his mother?
STAFFORD:	No—it's his wife!
BRICE:	Ohhhh.
MERE:	Say, Dick—I sure wish I could go along with you next week.
POWELL:	Be glad to have you, Meredith.
STAFFORD:	I know. Let's form a little party.
BRICE:	I wanna go to a party!
STAFFORD:	Oh, stop it. How about you coming along, Mary?
MARTIN:	Sounds good to me. I'm not very handy with a gun, though.
MERE:	Oh, I'll learn you how, Mary. I'm a regular ramrod.
POWELL:	Nimrod!
MERE:	I mean Nimrod. Pardon. (SIMPERS AT MARTIN)
BRICE:	He's dumb, ain't he, daddy?
MERE:	Oh, I suppose you're a smarty-pants! You're a dope!

BRICE: You're dopier than me. Ain't he, daddy?

STAFFORD: Snooks—you mean dopier than I!

BRICE: He's dopier than the both of us!

POWELL: Look, folks—if we're all going on a hunting trip let's not start fighting now.

MERE: (POUTING) Well, she started it.

PRICE: I did not! Sock him, daddy.

STAFFORD: Behave yourself, Snooks. Listen, fellows—I'll take her home and we'll make the arrangements later.

BRICE: I ain't going home.

STAFFORD: Why not?

BRICE: I wanna go hunting.

STAFFORD: You can't go with us.

BRICE: Why?

STAFFORD: Because it's too dangerous. You might get hit by a—hmmmm.

BRICE: What's the matter?

STAFFORD: Nothing. You can't go!

POWELL: You certainly wrestled with your conscience that time, daddy. Snooks—you be a good girl and stay home and we'll bring you a pair of tusks.

BRICE: What's tusks?

STAFFORD: Boar's teeth.

BRICE: What's a boar?

POWELL: A boar is a wild pig.

BRICE: Why is he wild?

POWELL: I don't know—he can't help it, I guess.

BRICE: Why?

POWELL: Take her, daddy.

STAFFORD: Listen, Snooks—you know what a boar is and you know what it looks like!

BRICE: No, I don't.

STAFFORD: You do too! I showed you a picture the other day of that wild looking, shaggy, ugly thing, with a snout and long protruding teeth!

BRICE: You mean Uncle Louie?

STAFFORD: Oh, come on! I'll see you later, Dick!

BRICE: Waaaaaahhhh. I wanna go hunting!

             (APPLAUSE)

At the Movies
(April 11, 1940)

MAXWELL HOUSE COFFEE TIME

April 11, 1940

POWELL: And now, ladies and gentlemen, here is Fanny Brice as Baby Snooks!

(MUSIC...APPLAUSE)

POWELL: Daddy, played by Hanley Stafford, has really let himself in for something. He promised to take Snooks to the movies—and since mother isn't home, he has to take little Robespierre along too. To make matters worse, the theatre is crowded and they have to wait for seats. As the scene opens we find them in the lobby—still waiting. Listen...

FATHER: Snooks—don't duck in and out like that. Stand next to me!

BRICE: Why?

FATHER: Because I don't want to lose our turn.

BRICE: I wanna sit down.

FATHER: In a couple of minutes. We can't sit down just yet.

BRICE: Why?

FATHER:	Because the house is jammed—and we have nothing to sit on.
BRICE:	I got something to—
FATHER:	Never mind that! We'll soon get seats.

(BABY STARTS TO CRY)

BRICE:	What's he bawling for?
FATHER:	He's hungry. Good thing I brought his bottle...Here Sweetie.

(BABY CRIES THEN GURGLES)

BRICE:	That's all he does. Eats, drinks and hollers!
FATHER:	You did the same things when you were his age! I hope he's quiet during the picture...Hmmm—he sure drained that bottle.
BRICE:	He's got an awful fat tummy, ain't he?
FATHER:	What of it?
BRICE:	Won't he make a wonderful policeman?
FATHER:	He's a good boy. Awful heavy though. Wonder how long we have to stand in the lobby.
BRICE:	Are we gonna see Shirley Temple?
FATHER:	Yes. And they have a fishing short here that I want to see.
BRICE:	Why?
FATHER:	I like fishing. Remember that time I went on a fishing trip? I brought home a sackful.
BRICE:	And mummy wouldn't let you bring them in the house.

FATHER:	Ahh—don't remind me of it! Such gorgeous fish! I had three halibut and one smelt.
BRICE:	They all smelt.
FATHER:	They did not! Anyway, I don't want to miss the fishing short.
BRICE:	I wanna see Shirley Temple.
FATHER:	You'll see her when she comes on the screen. She's in a wonderful picture.
BRICE:	What is it?
FATHER:	The Bluebird. It's a beautiful story and I know you'll love it.
BRICE:	Has it got kissing?
FATHER:	No!
BRICE:	Then I won't like it!
FATHER:	What kind of talk is that? This picture is especially for children.
BRICE:	I like Robert Taylor.
FATHER:	You would! Getting more like your mother every day!
BRICE:	Huh?
FATHER:	Nothing. If you don't enjoy this picture I'll be terribly disappointed.
BRICE:	Why?
FATHER:	Because it's one of the most beautiful fantasies ever written. It makes you forget about the world of tangibles.
BRICE:	I want one, daddy.

FATHER:	One what? I said tangibles—do you know what tangibles are?
BRICE:	Uh-huh. Little oranges.
FATHER:	That's tangerines!
BRICE:	I want a tangerine.
FATHER:	You can't have any tangerines! When we get seated I'll let you have a piece of candy.
BRICE:	Where's Shirley Temple?
FATHER:	I told you she's in the picture! You'll see her in a minute!
BRICE:	How will I know her when I see her?
FATHER:	When you see The Bluebird you'll know it's Shirley Temple.
BRICE:	Has she got a blue beard?
FATHER:	Yes—and a green mustache! The picture has nothing to do with blue beards! It's called the Bluebird.
BRICE:	Why?
FATHER:	Because it is! The Bluebird is the symbol of happiness and in the story the two children go searching for it.
	(BABY CRIES)
BRICE:	Is he hungry again?
FATHER:	He can't be. He just finished eight ounces of milk. What's the matter, baby?
	(BABY CRIES)
BRICE:	I know.

FATHER:	He's probably tired.
BRICE:	Did you bring along an extra—
FATHER:	Yes—I brought along an extra cookie!
BRICE:	That ain't what I—
FATHER:	You just mind your own business. I'll take care of Robespierre!
BRICE:	Is he gonna sit on your lap?
FATHER:	Of course he is. Why do you ask?
BRICE:	Oh, nothing...you're gonna be awful sorry you brought him.
FATHER:	Don't be silly—he'll sleep all thru the picture. There—he's quiet already. Wish they'd hurry with those seats!
BRICE:	I wanna see the picture!
FATHER:	Now, don't *you* start!
BRICE:	I wanna see Shirley Bluebeard!
FATHER:	Shh—the people are coming out! Come on—we can get seats now! Hang on to my coat.
BRICE:	It's dark in here.
FATHER:	(WHISPERS) Shh—don't make any noise.
BRICE:	Why?
FATHER:	Because you'll disturb the people watching the picture. Follow me.
BRICE:	I want some candy.
FATHER:	I can't give it to you now.

BRICE:	Why?
FATHER:	Because I've got my hands full!
BRICE:	Full of candy?
FATHER:	No—and keep quiet! I can't find any seats...Haven't they got an usher in this broken-down place!
GIRL:	How far down, please?
FATHER:	Oh. Anyplace around the middle.
BRICE:	Who's flashing that light, daddy?
FATHER:	Shh—it's the usher. She's going to show us to our seats.
BRICE:	Is she gonna sit with us?
FATHER:	No!
BRICE:	Why?
GIRL:	Watch your step, please. Here's two seats.
BRICE:	I wanna sit in the first row.
FATHER:	Oh, sit down!
BRICE:	This seat's too lumpy!
MAN:	Hey—get off my lap!
BRICE:	Oh, excuse me.
FATHER:	Snooks! Come here and sit down! Now, don't make a sound.
BRICE:	Awight...Daddy?
FATHER:	Shh—what is it?
BRICE:	Tell me a story.

FATHER:	Are you out of your mind? You're going to see Shirley Temple in a minute. Sit still—the picture will start as soon as this short is over.
BRICE:	What short?
FATHER:	The picture that's on now. That's the fishing short.
BRICE:	I can't see nothing.
FATHER:	Look at the screen. See those two men fishing? They're showing how to catch trout.
BRICE:	Why ain't they talking?
FATHER:	You don't talk when you fish.
BRICE:	Why?
FATHER:	(HISSES) I don't know—keep quiet! You're disturbing the people.
BRICE:	I wanna hear the men talk!
FATHER:	Maybe one of them will talk soon.
BRICE:	When?
FATHER:	Right away!
MAN:	Ahh—shut up with that racket!
BRICE:	Which one was that, daddy?
FATHER:	It was the man behind you. And if you don't keep quiet we'll have to leave! Watch the fishermen.
BRICE:	How is fishies born, daddy?
FATHER:	The fish lay eggs.
BRICE:	Like a chicken?

FATHER:	No. A chicken lays one egg at a time but a fish lays hundreds of eggs.
BRICE:	Why?
FATHER:	I don't know—but a single trout can lay ten thousand eggs a year!
BRICE:	A single trout?
FATHER:	Yes.
BRICE:	How about the married ones?
FATHER:	Shhhhh! Watch the picture.
BRICE:	Does fish cackle when they lay eggs?
FATHER:	No—only a hen cackles. The hen lays an egg then she cackles when the chick is born.
BRICE:	Who cackled when I was born?
FATHER:	Nobody!
BRICE:	Why?
FATHER:	Because you're not a chicken! A hen has to sit on an egg until it's hatched.
BRICE:	Did anybody sit on me?
FATHER:	No!
MAN:	Well, it would have been a great idea! Can't you keep that kid quiet, mister?
FATHER:	I'm sorry. You hear that, Snooks? You'll have to keep quiet!
BRICE:	Then tell me a story.

FATHER:	No!
BRICE:	Just a quiet little story.
FATHER:	If you make another sound I'll take you home!
BRICE:	Waaaahhhh!
FATHER:	All right—all right! Shhh! I'll tell you a quick story.
MAN:	I'll tell her a story! Did you ever hear the one about the kid who wanted a sock and finally got it in the end?
BRICE:	No.
MAN:	Well—that's where you'll get it if you don't keep quiet!
FATHER:	Now, just a minute –
MAN:	I paid two bits to see a picture and I'm gonna see it in peace!
FATHER:	That's all right! She's my child and I'll handle her!
BRICE:	Sock him, daddy!
FATHER:	You keep still!
	(BABY STARTS TO HOLLER)
GIRL:	I'm sorry, but you'll have to stop this noise or leave the theatre.
MAN:	It's that kid! She needs a good licking! And I'll let her have it in a minute!
FATHER:	Is that so! Nobody spanks my kid—understand!
BRICE:	(LAUGHS) Tell him, daddy!
FATHER:	Nobody but me! (SLAP)

BRICE:	Waaaaaahhhhh!
	(BABY HOLLERS)
FATHER:	Let's get out of here! And they say there's peace in America!
BRICE:	WAAAAAHHHHHH!
	(MUSIC...APPLAUSE)
POWELL:	That was wonderful, Mary! And now, we continue with—
STAFFORD:	Say, Dick!
POWELL:	Oh, hello, Daddy. Feeling better?
STAFFORD:	Fine, thanks. What's this I hear about Meredith being a character reader?
POWELL:	Oh, I don't know. I guess he's picked up some book on the subject. Are you interested in it?
STAFFORD:	Well, in a way. Of course, most of my research has been in child psychology.
POWELL:	Oh, of course. I can see it's helped you immeasurably with Snooks.
STAFFORD:	What do you mean?
BRICE:	Yeah—what do you mean?
POWELL:	Now, don't gang up on me. I didn't say anything.
MARTIN:	Oh, hello, everybody.
STAFFORD:	Hello, Mary. Snooks—say hello to Miss Martin.
BRICE:	Hello, Mrs. Martin.

MARTIN: Hello, Snooks. Say—Meredith gave me the most wonderful reading!

STAFFORD: Character reading?

MARTIN: No—he told my fortune.

POWELL: Oh, he's branching out already. Hey—Meredith!

MERE: Okay, Dick. I've got you all figured out, now.

BRICE: What's he doing, Daddy?

STAFFORD: Shhh! I don't know.

MERE: Dick I can't possibly give you a character reading tonight.

POWELL: No time?

MERE: No. No character.

POWELL: Thanks.

STAFFORD: Look here, Meredith—can you tell anything from my face?

BRICE: I can tell, daddy.

STAFFORD: You stay out of this! What do you say, Meredith.

MERE: Well—let me see. What would you call that nose?

BRICE: Big!

STAFFORD: Keep quiet!

MERE: I guess it's the conservative type. Hmm—very conflicting. If I didn't know that you played poker a good deal—I'd say you were a man of regular habits.

BRICE:	That's one of his regular habits.
STAFFORD:	It is not! And you behave yourself!
BRICE:	I ain't doing nothing.
POWELL:	Let's see you use a little child psychology on her, daddy.
STAFFORD:	I would give her a spanking—but she hasn't had supper yet.
POWELL:	What's that got to do with it?
STAFFORD:	Well—I don't like to spank her on an empty stomach.
BRICE:	No—he always turns me over.
POWELL:	Maybe there are times when a different method would help, daddy.
STAFFORD:	Oh, by all means. As a matter of fact, I very seldom lose my temper with her. I find that a soft word gets much better results.
MERE:	Say, Daddy! Get Snooks away from my music!
STAFFORD:	(HOLLERS) Snooks! Take your hands off that music or I'll tan your hide!
POWELL:	I see what you mean, daddy.
BRICE:	I wanna go home, daddy.
STAFFORD:	In a few minutes, Snooks—I want to talk to Mr. Powell.
BRICE:	Why?
STAFFORD:	Because we're discussing something. Sit on Meredith's stool—and don't touch the music.
BRICE:	Awight.

FATHER:	I'll show you something, Dick. Here's a wonderful little test in child psychology. Come here, Meredith.
MERE:	What are you gonna do?
FATHER:	I'll show you why children are so hard to manage. Did you ever hear of defensive lying?
POWELL:	No.
FATHER:	Well—listen. Snooks—come here.
BRICE:	Yes, daddy?
FATHER:	(SUDDENLY) Who wrote Hamlet?
BRICE:	Waaaaahhhhh!
FATHER:	What are you yelling about?
BRICE:	I didn't do it!
FATHER:	There you are, fellows! What did I tell you!
MERE:	How do you like that! I'll bet she did it all the time!
POWELL:	Oh, what's the use?
FATHER:	I'll see you later. Come on, Snooks.
BRICE:	Goodbye, everybody! (LAUGHS)
POWELL:	I guess that just about settles child psychology for tonight. And to bring us back to normal, Meredith gives us his orchestra supplemented by the chorus in a special arrangement of "How High the Moon." Maestro!
	"HOW HIGH THE MOON"... ORCHESTRA:
	(APPLAUSE)

Magician
(April 18, 1940)

MAXWELL HOUSE COFFEE TIME
April 18, 1940

POWELL: And now, ladies and gentlemen, here is Fanny Brice as Baby Snooks!

(MUSIC...APPLAUSE)

Daddy, played by Hanley Stafford has a new hobby. He recently became very interested in magic and joined an amateur magicians society. Tonight they are giving a private performance and Daddy is going to entertain— so we find him preparing his bag of tricks and getting ready to leave. Listen.

FATHER: Guess I have everything...Folding flowers—disappearing cane—cards—changing bag. Hmm-mmm. Where's my wand?

BRICE: Hello, daddy.

FATHER: Oh. I didn't think I could get away without you snooping around.

BRICE: What you hiding in the bag, daddy?

FATHER: It's nothing to do with you. Go to bed. It's terribly late.

BRICE: What time is it?

FATHER: It's—it's one o'clock in the morning!

BRICE: No it ain't.

FATHER: What do you mean it ain't! Do you doubt my word?

BRICE: Uh-huh. Let me see your watch.

FATHER: No! If I tell you it's one o'clock it's one o'clock!

           (CLOCK CHIMES EIGHT)

FATHER: Darn fire engines! Go on to sleep!

BRICE: I wanna see what you got in the bag.

FATHER: You keep your hands off that bag!

BRICE: Why?

FATHER: Because it contains things you're not supposed to see!

BRICE: Then I wanna see 'em!

FATHER: This bag is full of magic secrets that I can't expose. Now do you understand why I can't let you look in the bag?

BRICE: Uh-huh. 'Cause it's full of something else!

FATHER: It is not! You know I belong to a magicians society!

BRICE: Why?

FATHER: Because that's my hobby—magic. A man's entitled to have a hobby, isn't he?

BRICE: Oh—I know what you got in the bag!

FATHER: What?

BRICE:	I ain't telling! But—I know!
FATHER:	You silly little thing! You make everything I do look so guilty!
BRICE:	I know!
FATHER:	Oh, stop it! I'm getting out of here! A man can't have a hobby!
BRICE:	Has Uncle Louie got a hobby?
FATHER:	Certainly! Uncle Louie etches.
BRICE:	Huh?
FATHER:	I said he etches!
BRICE:	Why don't he scratch himself?
FATHER:	Goodnight!
BRICE:	Where you going, daddy?
FATHER:	I told you—to the magicians society! There's a big dinner and entertainment—and I'm late now!
BRICE:	Are you a magician, daddy?
FATHER:	Just about the best in the world, that's all. If I wasn't in such a hurry I'd show you some wonderful tricks.
BRICE:	Do one trick.
FATHER:	No—I haven't got time.
BRICE:	Make me disappear.
FATHER:	I can't.
BRICE:	Why?

FATHER:	Don't worry—I'm working on it! Now go to bed.
BRICE:	I wanna go with you.
FATHER:	Do you realize what time it is? When I was your age I used to go to sleep with the chickens!
BRICE:	Every night?
FATHER:	Every single night!
BRICE:	Could you lay an egg?
FATHER:	Of course not!
BRICE:	Then why did you go to sleep with the chickens?
FATHER:	Because my father made me!
BRICE:	Wouldn't he let you sleep in the house?
FATHER:	Certainly I slept in the house.
BRICE:	Well, where did the chickens sleep?
FATHER:	We didn't have any chickens!
BRICE:	Then how did you sleep with them?
FATHER:	I slept alone!
BRICE:	Why?
FATHER:	Now you go right to bed before I spank you!
BRICE:	I wanna sleep with some chickens!
FATHER:	Oh—this is pretty kettle of fish!
BRICE:	I wanna sleep with some chickens and fish.
FATHER:	Snooks—I told you I'm in a hurry to get out of here! The magic society can't start without me!

BRICE: Why?

FATHER: Because we have a famous guest of honor who's going to be the toastmaster and I'm the chairman!

BRICE: What does the chairman do?

FATHER: He sits on the chair!

BRICE: Does the toastmaster sit on the toast?

FATHER: No! I'll tell you all about it in the morning.

BRICE: Do a trick, daddy.

FATHER: All right. Where's my cards?...Here—you see this card?

BRICE: Uh-huh.

FATHER: What is it?

BRICE: Uncle Louie.

FATHER: It's not Uncle Louie—it's the King of Spades! I'm going to change it to the King of Hearts.

BRICE: Why?

RATHER: You want to see a trick, don't you?

BRICE: Uh-huh.

FATHER: Well, I'm going to change this king from one suit to another.

BRICE: I don't see no suit.

FATHER: Listen, there are four kings and they're all of different suits.

BRICE: With pants?

FATHER:	No pants! These little designs are called suits so you can distinguish one from the other.
BRICE:	Who can?
FATHER:	The people who play cards!
BRICE:	Without pants?
FATHER:	Nobody plays cards without pants!
BRICE:	Why?
FATHER:	Do you want to see this trick or not?
BRICE:	I wanna see it.
FATHER:	Well, watch me closely—and keep your eye on the King of Spades. Presto—changeo! It is now the King of Hearts! (LAUGHS) How's that?
BRICE:	(SAME LAUGH) No good.
FATHER:	What's the matter with it?
BRICE:	Where's the bunny?
FATHER:	Bunny? What are you talking about?
BRICE:	Let me see you turn it into a bunny.
FATHER:	What for?
BRICE:	I wanna eat it.
FATHER:	I'm getting out of here—goodnight!
BRICE:	Waaaahhh!
FATHER:	What are you yelling about?
BRICE:	I wanna see a trick.

FATHER:	I just showed you one!
BRICE:	Show me another one!
FATHER:	All right—but then I leave—understand?
BRICE:	Understand.
FATHER:	Okay. Now—see this watch? I'm going to make it vanish into thin air. I hold it in my left hand—so! Then I pass my right hand over it—so! Now—you see my left hand is empty?
BRICE:	Uh-huh.
FATHER:	Then I must have the watch in my closed right hand.
BRICE:	Let me see it.
FATHER:	I'm not finished yet! I have the watch in my right hand—and I throw it right thru the closed window! Zing! My hand is empty!
BRICE:	Where's the watch!
FATHER:	I shall now make the watch reappear! I make a few passes—the window rises invisibly—the watch returns—and you'll find it in your pocket! Is it there?
BRICE:	(LAUGHS) I got it!
FATHER:	Pretty good, eh? Let me have the watch.
BRICE:	I throw it thru the closed window—(GLASS CRASH)—
FATHER:	Snooks!
BRICE:	Make it come back, daddy.

FATHER: Now, look what you've done! You threw my watch out of the window.

BRICE: Look in your pocket—maybe it came back.

FATHER: Ahhh—I should have known better than to start with you! Go to bed!

BRICE: I don't wanna.

FATHER: Snooks—I'm warning you! I have to go to the Magicians Society and I'm late now!

BRICE: If you do one more trick I'll let you go.

FATHER: I'll do a trick and you won't sit down for a week!

BRICE: Waaahhh!

FATHER: All right—all right! I'll do a trick with silks!

BRICE: No—do a trick with that big box.

FATHER: That's an escape trunk. I haven't got it finished yet.

BRICE: Make something disappear in it.

FATHER: No! It takes too long to get out and I—hmmm. Wait a minute.

BRICE: What are you looking at me for?

FATHER: I'm going to let you help me with this trunk trick, Snooks.

BRICE: Who, me?

FATHER: Yes. Get in—I'll show you how to escape from it.

BRICE: You do it first.

FATHER:	All right—I'll show you how easy it is. Here—I'll climb in. Now—when I close this lid—you turn the key and lock it.
BRICE:	Awight.
FATHER:	Then count five and I'll be out! Ready?
BRICE:	Ready.
FATHER:	Okay—close the lid!
	(LID CLOSES)
BRICE:	Shall I lock it now, daddy?
FATHER:	(MUFFLED) Yes. And turn around so you can't see how I get out.
	(KEY TURNS IN LOCK)
BRICE:	It's locked, daddy.
FATHER:	(MUFFLED) Start counting!
BRICE:	One - two - three - four - five! Are you out?
FATHER:	(MUFFLED) Just a second—this broken-down gimmick is stuck! Count again.
BRICE:	One - two - three - four - five.
FATHER:	(MUFFLED) Something's wrong! I can't slide the panel.
	(THUMPING NOISE)
BRICE:	One - two three four five!
	(THUMPING NOISE)

FATHER:	(MUFFLED) Snooks—open the lock.
BRICE:	I throw the key thru the closed window—(GLASS CRASH)
FATHER:	(THUMPING) Get me out of here!
BRICE:	I ain't got the key, daddy.
FATHER:	(MUFFLED) Where is it?
BRICE:	I threw it out the window. Look in your pocket.
FATHER:	(MUFFLED) Snooks! Go get that key! Get me out of here!
BRICE:	I'm going to bed. Goodnight, daddy!
FATHER:	(MUFFLED SCREAMING) Don't you dare! I'll rip this trunk to pieces.
	(SPLINTERING CRASH)
BRICE:	Is that the trick, daddy?
FATHER:	No: Here's the trick! See my right hand? It's empty, isn't it?
BRICE:	Uh-huh.
FATHER:	Now I put a slipper in it—
BRICE:	I can't see it.
FATHER:	You don't have to see it.
BRICE:	Why?
FATHER:	Because you're going to feel it! You little—(SLAP)
BRICE:	Waaaahhhhhhh!

(MUSIC...APPLAUSE)

POWELL: Thank you, Baby Snooks and Daddy! Now, here's lovely Jary Martin again—and she's going to sing something out of the ordinary. A special arrangement of the classic "Il Bacio." Mary—did you have any particular reason for choosing that number?

MARTIN: No. I just like it, that's all.

POWELL: That's good enough reason for me. No more subtleties tonight! Ladies and gentlemen—Mary Martin singing—"Il Bacio."

"IL BACIO"—MARTIN & ORCHESTRA

(APPLAUSE)

POWELL: That was splendid, Mary. And now we continue with—

(PHONE RINGS)

POWELL: Hello. Yes. Yes. Just a minute, Mrs. Higgins...Oh, Daddy!

STAFF: Yes, Dick?

POWELL: Phone for you. The missus.

STAFF: Oh. Hello?...Yes...Yes...Oh. Are you sure?...Hmm—okay I'll let her know...She's going to holler plenty...Okay... Goodbye.

POWELL: Anything?

STAFF: Just a little more trouble for the old man, that's all. Snooks has had a pet turtle for about six months—and my wife says she just found it floating on its back. I've got to tell the kid.

POWELL:	Think she'll take it hard, Daddy?
STAFF:	Oh, well—you know kids. Of course it's only a turtle and—
MERE:	Say, Daddy—why don't you let me tell her? I'm very diplomatic!
POWELL:	Sure—he'll sit and stare at her. He's very subtle!
STAFF:	I don't know—she'll only fight with me.
POWELL:	Better let me handle it. Shh—here she comes now.
BRICE:	Daddy! I wanna go home.
STAFF:	Just a minute, Snooks. Mr. Powell wants to talk to you.
BRICE:	Why?
POWELL:	Well, Snooks—I—er—you—er. Let me see. Suppose you had a turtle.
BRICE:	I got a turtle. His name is Foop and he can stretch his nose. (LAUGHS) Ain't he funny?
STAFF:	Go ahead, Dick. Stab her while she's laughing.
POWELL:	Yes. Well, he—or—this morning... I—er—
MERE:	Oh, I can't stand this. Snooks—you got a dead turtle, haven't you?
BRICE:	No, I got a live one.
MERE:	What'll you bet?
STAFF:	What a diplomat! Snooks—now don't get excited.
BRICE:	What happened to Foop?

MERE: He got bumped off. He's finished.

BRICE: Waaahhhhh!

STAFF: Shh! Snooks - don't carry on like that. It's only a turtle. I'll get you another one.

BRICE: Waaahhhhh!

POWELL: Oh, Snooks—now take it easy. I wouldn't cry that way.

BRICE: You can cry any way you like—this is my way! Waaaahhhh!

FATHER: Wait a minute, Snooks. Just a minute—I got a wonderful idea.

BRICE: Waaahhhhh!

FATHER: Oh, stop it!

BRICE: Huh?

FATHER: I know you feel bad, but here's what we'll do. The turtle is gone, see? We can't bring him back—so we'll give him a lovely funeral.

BRICE: Funeral?

FATHER: That's it! Only instead of being a sad affair—we'll build a bright colored little box to bury him in—we'll invite a lot of children from the neighborhood—

BRICE: Uh-huh.

FATHER: I'll provide plenty of cake and ice-cream - and each child can bring a pretty flower.

BRICE: For Foop?

FATHER:	Sure. I may even lot you stay home from school that day—and right after the lovely ceremony—why, I'll get you another turtle.
BRICE:	Ohh.

(PHONE RINGS)

POWELL:	Hello…Oh. Here, Daddy.
STAFF:	Hello. Oh! Fine! Okay. Snooks—you don't have to worry any more.
BRICE:	Why?
STAFF:	Mother just called—the turtle's alive!
BRICE:	Waaaaaahhhhh!
STAFF:	What are you yelling about?
BRICE:	Bump him off so we can have that funeral!
STAFF:	Ahhh—what's the use! Come on—let's go home!
BRICE:	Waaaahhhhh!

(APPLAUSE)

Partial Notes & Script for a Baby Snooks Show

It's two o'clock in the morning and Daddy is fast asleep - but Snooks is not... She has learned that daybreak will bring Daddy's birthday, and she, for one, doesn't intend to let him go unrewarded. When we find her she's in the kitchen busily preparing to bake a chocolate layer cake.

She has the cookbook turned to the necessary recipe, and all the ingredients are spread out before her. She makes a mess of things - throwing in eggshells, etc - but it isn't until the explosion that Daddy awakens. It seems that Snooks had first turned the oven on to get it hot, but didn't remember to light it until five minutes later.

Daddy comes racing downstairs forgetting to put on his slippers - it isn't until he walks into the guck on the kitchen floor that he remembers. Daddy demands to know the reason for the explosion and Snooks tells him her cake has fallen. He's all set to let her have it, when she explains that she was baking a cake in honor of his birthday. This softens daddy up, and he abandons the idea of licking her in order to teach her the proper manner to bake a chocolate layer cake. It seems that before he was married had a quite a reputation as an amateur chef.

He proceeds with his baking - first lining up the necessary stuff and adding a few more of his own. Then he proceeds to explain the process. "First", he says, "you knead the dough." Snooks wants to know what he needs it for. He tells her that he kneads the dough for the cake. She wants to know how much he's charging. "It's not that kind of dough," he tells her. "It's batter." "Batter than what?" she demands.

ANNOUNCER: It's two o'clock in the morning and Daddy is fast asleep - but Snooks is not. She has learned that daybreak will bring Daddy's birthday, and she, for one, doesn't intend to let him go unrewarded. Right now she's in the kitchen busily preparing to bake a cake. Let's look in:

BRICE: (To "PONY BOY") Chocolate cake, chocolate cake, I'm gonna bake a chocolate cake. Now lemme see. (READS) Melt chocolate and butter over slow fire… Slow fire – hmmm – I better turn on the gas now and light it later. (CLICK) Now - take three eggs and break them in a mixing bowl - now I break 'em! (SOUND OF EGGS SPLATTERING) That's that. Now I take half a cup of butter - and melt over slow fire – ooh, I better light the oven now. (SOUND OF MATCH BEING STRUCK. HOLLOW EXPLOSION) Oh-oh!

FATHER: (OFF MIKE) Snooks! Snooks! What was that?

BRICE: My cake fell!

FATHER: What cake?

BRICE: The cake I was making for your birthday.

FATHER: Well, I'll teach you to - My birthday? Oh… What kind of cake were your making, Snooks?

BRICE: I was gonna make you a chocolate layer cake with fifty candles.

FATHER: Fifty? But I'm only forty-six.

BRICE: No, you ain't.

BRICE:	All right, forty-seven. (Kid's got a memory like an elephant.)
BRICE:	Mommy said you're forty-nine.
DADDY:	Oh, she did, did she?
BRICE:	Yes, she did she. Daddy, how old is Mommy?
FATHER:	She's fifty-four! (There - I guess that'll teach her a lesson.)
BRICE:	How old are you, Daddy?
FATHER:	I've already told you - I'm forty-seven! I was born in 1893, and you can figure it out yourself.
BRICE:	(MUMBLES)
FATHER:	What are you doing?
BRICE:	I'm figuring.
FATHER:	Well, how old am I?
BRICE:	You're forty-nine.
FATHER:	1893 to 1940 is forty-seven. Where did you get 49?
BRICE:	Mommy told me!
FATHER:	Oh, stop making me feel old.
BRICE:	Daddy.
FATHER:	What?
BRICE:	When was I born?
FATHER:	I don't know.
BRICE:	You don't know when I was born?

FATHER:	Oh - I thought you said WHY... You were born in 1933.
BRICE:	How do you know?
FATHER:	MOMMY TOLD ME! Now where's the recipe you were cooking from?
BRICE:	In this book, Daddy. Can you make a cake?
FATHER:	Can I make a cake? (LAUGHS) Why, ten years ago I was elected best all-around chef by the women's auxiliary club of Azusa. What do you think of that?
BRICE:	Can you crochet, too?
FATHER:	Never mind that. Hand me that book. Now let me see - chocolate muffins, chocolate eclairs - ahhh, here's chocolate cake.
BRICE:	Gimme a piece.
FATHER:	It's only the recipe! First we have to get all the ingredients together – like flour eggs, milk - then we knead the dough.
BRICE:	What do we need it for?
FATHER:	It's not that kind of dough. It's batter.
BRICE:	Batter than what?
FATHER:	Stop trying to be funny and hand me a couple of those eggs.
BRICE:	Which couple?
FATHER:	Any couple. Don't tell me you don't know what a couple is.
BRICE:	Awight, I won't tell you.

FATHER:	Look - there are four eggs. Now, if you take two away, how many are left?
BRICE:	None.
FATHER:	Oh, no! If you take two away from four, two are left. Isn't that so?
BRICE:	No.
FATHER:	Why not?
BRICE:	Cause you took two away.
FATHER:	But I left two. How many eggs are there altogether?
BRICE:	Six.
FATHER:	There are four. Count them - one, two, three, four. Now where are the other two you're talking about?
BRICE:	You're sitting on 'em.
FATHER:	What!
BRICE:	(LAUGHS) April Fool!
FATHER:	April Fool in May! Now listen, Snooks, if you make another sound I'm gonna send you to bed without letting you watch me bake this cake.
BRICE:	I wanna go to bed!
FATHER:	You can't go to bed - you've gotta stay here and help me! Now get me a teaspoon of vanilla.
BRICE:	Vanilla what?
FATHER:	Just plain vanilla - vanilla vanilla.
BRICE:	What kind of cake we making, Daddy?

FATHER:	Chocolate cake.
BRICE:	Huh?
FATHER:	I'm putting the vanilla in to give it a flavor.
BRICE:	Vanilla flavor?
FATHER:	No, chocolate flavor!
BRICE:	Well, why don't you put chocolate in?
FATHER:	I'm going to make the chocolate out of the vanilla! Now you know what I'm gonna do with this empty pan?
BRICE:	Uh-huh - you gonna make a rabbit jump out of it.
FATHER	I'm going to make a chocolate filling. Look up the recipe, Snooks.
BRICE:	I thought you -
FATHER:	I know how - I just want to see if they're making it the same way these days. Have you got it?
BRICE:	Uh-huh.
FATHER:	What does it say?
BRICE:	(READS) Put chocolate filling No. 3, page 436, in pan and -
FATHER:	Well, get me page 436.

(SOUND OF PAPER BEING TORN)

BRICE:	HERE!
FATHER:	You didn't have to tear it out of the book!

C Note
(story treatment)

Baby Snooks Treatment

Daddy's playing solitaire when Snooks busts in on him.

He tries to get rid of her, but no dice - he agrees to let her stay if she doesn't utter a sound. She keeps perfectly still - for about two seconds, and then aggravates him into explaining the intricacies of solitaire. He finally gives up the game after she catches him cheating for about the third time.

He's about to give her a going over when he notices something she has clutched tightly in one hand. She won't show it to him - wants him to guess what it is. So Daddy starts guessing - he guesses everything from a lollipop to an elephant but according to her he's colder than a well-digger's bazola.

Under threat of walloping Snooks confesses that she has a one hundred dollar bill in her paw - and now Daddy's really gonna give it to her - that is, until he discovers that she really has a hundred dollar bill.

He inspects the C note, finds it legit, and asks her where she got it. She tells him that she was a very good girl in school today, and since they ran out of gold stars, they gave her the bill instead. He questions her further, but all he can get out of her is four or five very big whoppers.

Daddy goes thru all kinds of torture wondering whether he should turn it over to the police or keep it. Considers taking ad out in the newspaper (Might do gag about Owners please form a line, etc.) but drops that thought when he realizes it's gonna cost him money.

Daddy, although he won't admit it, is doping out every angle as to how he can keep the tin - but the thought that he might get into a jam is holding him back. He decides to arrange his alibi right now so he won't get into trouble later.

(He enacts the possible outcome, with Snooks as the Judge and himself as the defendant.)

After that hectic little scene he decides that he wouldn't be found dead with the dough. He hands the bill back to her and tells her to take it and place it in the exact spot she found it. He follows, and we discover that she's taken the money out of Daddy's drawer.

If you wanna make this spot a running theme, you can finish with Daddy still having the C note in his possession, and still undecided about what to do with it. Next week you can open with Daddy reading the "Lost and Found" columns and finding one stating that a hundred dollar bill had been lost, etc. Takes Snooks along to interview the advertiser.

Thanksgiving

"SNOOKS"

FATHER: Snooks, stop fooling with that pen and ink—you've got the ink all over your dress. What on earth are you doing?

BRICE: I wanna write Santa Claus a letter.

FATHER: This is no time to write Santa Claus a letter. Christmas is six weeks away. Next week is Thanksgiving.

BRICE: What's Thanksgiving?

FATHER: That's a holiday when we all give thanks for everything we've received during the year.

BRICE: I didn't receive nothing.

FATHER: Now Snooks, you've got a lot to be thankful for. You're living in a nice home, and you've got nice food. When I was your age I didn't have such good food.

BRICE: Aren't you glad you're living with us now?

FATHER: You don't understand, Snooks—I'm going to prepare a beautiful banquet for Thanksgiving. Did you see the nice live turkey we have in the back yard?

BRICE: Uh-huh.

FATHER:	Well, that's one thing we all of us should be thankful for—that we can afford to kill such a nice big turkey for Thanksgiving.
BRICE:	All of us should be thankful?
FATHER:	Of course.
BRICE:	The turkey, too?
FATHER:	Stop asking foolish questions.
BRICE:	Why?
FATHER:	Snooks, put that pen and ink down. You'll make a mess of yourself.
BRICE:	I wanna write Santa Claus a letter.
FATHER:	I told you this isn't Christmas.
BRICE:	When is Christmas?
FATHER:	After Thanksgiving.
BRICE:	Waaaaahhh!
FATHER:	What are you crying about?
BRICE:	I want Christmas to come first.
FATHER:	Why?
BRICE:	So I'll get something to be thankful for.
FATHER:	Look Snooks, you can't change holidays around.
BRICE:	What's holidays?
FATHER:	Well, people make holidays to celebrate big events, like George Washington's birthday is a holiday—Lincoln's birthday is a holiday.

BRICE: Why was they born on holidays?

FATHER: They weren't born on holidays.

BRICE: You just said they was.

FATHER: No—no—they were born on ordinary days, but after they became famous, the people made them holidays, so little girls like you could stay home from school and celebrate. Is that clear?

BRICE: Uh-huh...Daddy!

FATHER: What?

BRICE: I don't wanna go to school tomorrow.

FATHER: Why not?

BRICE: 'Cause I just made a holiday.

FATHER: You made a holiday? What are you going to celebrate?

BRICE: My pussycat's birthday!

FATHER: Ridiculous! A national holiday is only for a great event. What did your pussy cat do that she deserves a national holiday?

BRICE: She had six kittens.

FATHER: There's nothing remarkable about that.

BRICE: Can you do it?

FATHER: Listen, Snooks, I've been trying to explain to you that a national holiday must be some great occasion like Thanksgiving.

BRICE: What's Thanksgiving?

FATHER:	That's to celebrate the landing of the Pilgrims on Plymouth Rock.
BRICE:	Is that in Europe?
FATHER:	No—no—that's in this country.
BRICE:	What's in this country?
FATHER:	PLYMOUTH ROCK! The Pilgrims landed on the rock, after they had travelled on the ocean for six weeks.
BRICE:	Who travelled?
FATHER:	The Pilgrims!! You see, today we cross the ocean in four days, but at that time the Pilgrims stayed on the ocean for six long weeks.
BRICE:	Why—didn't they want to get off it?
FATHER:	Of course they wanted to, but they couldn't.
BRICE:	Who couldn't?
FATHER:	The Pilgrims!!!
BRICE:	What Pilgrims?
FATHER:	The Pilgrims—the people who first came here.
BRICE:	Here in this house?
FATHER:	No—the rock! The rock that they landed on!
BRICE:	The rock that landed on the Pilgrims?
FATHER:	No—the Pilgrims that landed on the rock! Plymouth Rock!
BRICE:	Is that in Europe?

FATHER:	No! No! A thousand times no!
BRICE:	Is that in Africa?
FATHER:	Of course not!
BRICE:	I know where the rock is.
FATHER:	Where?
BRICE:	You got it in your pocket!
FATHER:	Nonsense! It's a very big rock—200 people landed on it. And for days they walked about looking for food.
BRICE:	Where? On the rock?
FATHER:	No—in the woods. They came to a clearing—they built cabins and all their food supplies gave out and they were about to starve when one of the Pilgrims rushed in with the thing we all eat for Thanksgiving now. And what do you think that was?
BRICE:	I know—the rock!
FATTER:	No, no. A turkey! Is that clear?
BRICE:	Uh-huh.
FATHER:	Have you any questions?
BRICE:	Yeah.
FATHER:	What is it?
BRICE:	Now can I write my letter to Santa Claus?
FATHER:	Oh, what's the use? Go ahead, write your letter and hurry up so we can get out of here and go to the movies.
BRICE:	Awight... Daddy!

FATHER:	What?
BRICE:	Is grandma in the next room?
FATHER:	Yes, grandma is in the next room. Why do you ask?
BRICE:	She said Santa Claus would give me anything I wanted for Christmas.
FATHER:	All right, dictate your letter to Santa Claus, and I'll write it so we can get out of here.
BRICE:	Awight... "Dear Santa Claus—"
FATHER:	I've got it—"Dear Santa Claus—"
BRICE:	Send me a bi-i-ig white horsie - (SHOUTS) A B-I-I-I-G WHITE HORSIE.
FATHER:	Why do you shout like that—Santa Claus isn't deaf.
BRICE:	I know—but grandma is!

BUSINESS: APPLAUSE...

Treasure
(story treatment)

Daddy's trying to get some much-needed rest when Snooks busts in on him singing "Yo Ho Ho and a bottle of Rum, etc." Snooks is a pretty bedraggled-looking kid and Daddy wants to know what she could have been doing to get herself so dirty. She tells him that she she's been playing Pirate - and she's been playing it in the backyard. She's been digging, so that explains the dirt. He then wants to know what she expected to find in the backyard - and when she tells him "Gold," he laughs loudly, but not for long. Upon further investigation he finds that she's really discovered gold - a gold watch - and to make matters worse, it's Daddy's. At the moment it's not in very good condition - the glass is gone, the case is busted and as Snooks puts it, "I took the hands off so they wouldn't get dirty." The machinery of the watch seems to have disappeared in the shuffle, too - but Daddy tells her not to worry, as he will give her the works later.

It seems that she had been digging in the yard for a while, but it became dull because the only thing she could discover was two snails and a stale worm. These, she explains, she put in Daddy's coat pocket for safe-keeping. The watch is easy to explain, too - she simply took it out from Daddy's bureau and buried it - first thoughtfully wrapping it in one of Daddy's shirts to keep it from getting soiled - then she tried to forget where she hid it, so she could have the pleasant surprise of making a unexpected discovery. But alas, altho she buried it three or four times she always remembered where it was.

To help herself forget, she continues, she has also buried a pair of Daddy's shoes - figuring that this would help confuse her a bit. While Daddy holds his breath, and his temper, she assures him that it didn't work - she still remembered where the watch was. So, she continues, she dug up the watch once more - but this time she had forgotten where the shoes were. So she buried Daddy's bathrobe and hat to help her remember. Daddy, fearful that her memory might have become bad enough to bury little Robespierre, rushes quickly for a shovel, but she intercepts him and confesses that she's been lying about the whole thing.

Daddy's so relieved, he forgets about the broken watch. Snooks takes advantage of the situation and prevails upon him to tell her a Pirate Story. He tells her the story of "Captain Kidd" - and after many interruptions we tag with Daddy remembering his broken watch and acting accordingly.

Telling Time

SNOOKS

FATHER: Snooks—Tonight I'm going to teach you how to tell time.

BRICE: Ooooh—That's nice.

FATHER: I'm glad you like the idea.

BRICE: What ideal?

FATHER: The idea about telling time.

BRICE: What's time, daddy?

FATHER: Time is the twenty-four hours in the day.

BRICE: What day, daddy?

FATHER: Any day—now to tell time—

BRICE: Is it a story?

FATHER: Of course not.

BRICE: When you tell a story, you say once upon a time.

FATHER: This is entirely different.

BRICE: Why?

FATHER:	Because in that instance "time" does not mean "time" by hours and minutes.
BRICE:	Time don't mean time?
FATHER:	Not as you used it.
BRICE:	Then what does it mean?
FATHER:	I just told you it means time by hours and minutes.
BRICE:	Oh-hoh.
FATHER:	Well, I'm glad you're beginning to understand.
BRICE:	Understand what?
FATHER:	The difference in time.
BRICE:	What's the difference?
FATHER:	Snooks, you're not paying attention. Now you must learn to tell time. You're old enough to know whether it's morning - noon - or night.
BRICE:	I know now, daddy.
FATHER:	You do?
BRICE:	Yes. When you get up, it's afternoon. When I go to bed, it's night, and when you come home, it's morning.
FATHER:	Never mind that. Here, look at my watch.
BRICE:	Oo-oo… it's pretty.
FATHER:	Well thanks, Snooks.
BRICE:	For what, daddy?
FATHER:	Oh sometimes you're impossible! Now, this is the face.

BRICE:	The face?
FATHER:	Yes, the face of the watch.
BRICE:	Where's the mouth?
FATHER:	A watch doesn't have a mouth.
BRICE:	It's got a face, ain't it?
FATHER:	Of course it's got a face.
BRICE:	Then why ain't it got a mouth?
FATHER:	Because it hasn't, that's all.
BRICE:	Well, if it ain't got a mouth, how can it tell time?
FATHER:	It don't tell time.
BRICE:	Then what's it good for?
FATHER:	Snooks, don't ask such ridiculous questions—the face of a watch is where to put the hands.
BRICE:	What hands?
FATHER:	The hands of the watch!
BRICE:	Has it got hands?
FATHER:	Yes, it has hands and there they are!
BRICE:	They don't look like hands.
FATHER:	But nevertheless, they are hands.
BRICE:	Do they get dirty?
FATHER:	Of course not. They're covered with glass.
BRICE:	Daddy… can I have my hands covered with glass?

FATHER: Why on earth do you want your hands covered with glass?

BRICE: If they don't get dirty—I don't have to wash 'em.

FATHER: Snooks, I don't know what I'm ever going to do with you. Now listen. The hands move around on the face of the watch and you tell the time by their position.

BRICE: You can tell time by the hands on the face?

FATHER: That's it exactly.

BRICE: Look, daddy—I put my hands on my face—what time is it?

FATHER: Snooks—I'm trying to explain to you that a watch is a delicate piece of mechanism that ticks off the seconds, the seconds upon which every move is predicated.

BRICE: Do you feel alright, daddy?

FATHER: Yes, I feel great. Now Snooks, please pay attention.

BRICE: Alright, daddy.

FATHER: The little hand is the hour hand—and the big hand is the minute hand.

BRICE: The big one is the minute hand?

FATHER: Yes.

BRICE: Is a minute more than an hour?

FATHER: No, it's less.

BRICE: Then why is it the biggest hand?

FATHER:	Snooks, you're driving me crazy.
BRICE:	Why?
FATHER:	Because you ask such foolish questions.
BRICE:	What foolish questions?
FATHER:	What you're asking me.
BRICE:	What am I asking you?
FATHER:	Snooks, Snooks, stop it or I'll spank you within an inch of your life.
BRICE:	Wa-a-a—
FATHER:	What are you crying for? I haven't touched you yet!
BRICE:	Cause your face got so red—
FATHER:	Well, you're giving me high blood pressure.
BRICE:	What's high—
FATHER:	And don't ask me what high blood pressure is!
BRICE:	Why?
FATHER:	Snooks, if it's the last thing I do, I'm going to teach you to tell time.
BRICE:	I don't wanna learn—
FATHER:	Why don't you want to learn?
BRICE:	Because I ain't got a watch.
FATHER:	That's no excuse. If you don't learn how to tell time, how will you ever know what time it is?
BRICE:	I put a nickel in the telephone and somebody tells me.

Snooks Synopses
(story ideas)

One of the newspapers is sponsoring a beautiful Baby contest with a large cash prize to the one sending in the best photograph of their child.

Daddy has gone to quite a bit of expense in buying a camera, a developing outfit, enlarger and all sorts of films... He's even gone to the trouble of turning his study into a darkroom—so it's no wonder that Snooks is a little frightened when she enters... Daddy doesn't feel so good either, because Snooks' premature entrance let light into the room and ruined about fifteen bucks worth of film for Daddy.

Daddy explains that he had been taking pictures of Robespierre—tells her about the contest for beautiful babies—and naturally she wants him to enter her.

He explains the intricacies of film developing, camera parts, etc. and finally agrees to let her be his assistant when they take the next pictures of Robespierre.

He sends her upstairs to get Robespierre ready, and is a little perturbed to find that she has him strapped to a chair so he won't wiggle.

Daddy unstraps the baby and is all set to take the first picture when Snooks remarks that Robespierre doesn't exactly look up to par. Daddy figures that he could do with a little primping up—so he gets a pair of scissors and proceeds to trim the baby's hair... But according to Snooks' criticism it seems that Daddy can't get both sides of Robespierre's head even, and before he knows it he has cut off all of the kid's hair.

Snooks suggests that they make him a small toupee out of the mattress stuffing, but Daddy discards the idea and proceeds with his picture taking... Snooks keeps interfering and getting in the way, but after lots of trouble Daddy finally manages to take about eight different poses.

They head back for the dark room—Daddy quite confident that he has taken the winning pictures—but when he opens the camera he finds there was no film in it ... So for no good reason he spanks Snooks.

One of the picture studios has sent out a call for a baby to be used in a forthcoming flicker–they want a male, year old baby, and Daddy thinks that Robespierre will fill the bill–so we find them, and the inevitable Snooks, on one of the larger sound stages, waiting for a test.

The director is busy at the moment, directing a sequence wherein the distraught hero has come home to find that his wife has left him forever, and what's more, has taken the darling baby with her. His part, at this point, consists of one line—or rather, the repetition of one line—the line being "Oh—where is my baby! Oh—where is my baby!" ... Snooks, only trying to help, ruins the scene by hollering, "He's right here–chewing on Daddy's necktie!"

The director tears his hair, and tells Daddy in no uncertain terms that Snooks has ruined about two thousand feet... Snooks wants to know whose feet they are.

After a few more retakes, with Snooks constantly spoiling the shot, hollering that she wants to meet Donald Duck, or something—the director decides that he's gonna do this scene right this time, or die in the attempt—so they tie a gag around Snooks' mouth... Everything is in readiness, and the actor is about to recite his fateful lines once more, when the director decides he can soften up the scene a bit—he hollers for the electrician to "throw a baby on the hero"—and Snooks ruins another scene by trying to toss Robespierre at him... They call for a "Dolly" several times, and she tries to help here, too.

The director finally decides to delay the shooting for a while in order to give Robespierre his screen test... Here, we bring in a Makeup man—who decides that Robespierre is a little too bald for the part—and they compromise by making a small toupee for him.

In the test, Robespierre is called upon to shed a few tears, but despite the efforts of Daddy and the director—telling him sad things, etc.—the kid laughs... Just when they're about to give up, the kid lets go with a terrific bellow... The director hollers "Shoot him!" and Snooks spoils this one, in defense of her brother, by giving out with her own private holler—she didn't want him shot, she explains.

All is quiet once more, and their efforts to make Robespierre cry are proving unsuccessful—when miraculously the kid starts crying again—they find out later Snooks has been pinching him. Now they can't stop him from crying—and Daddy, being a bit of a ham, suggests they let him in the picture, too, and he'll keep Robespierre quiet... He gets the kid quiet and the scene is about to be shot when Snooks starts hollering—she wants her picture taken, too.

The director decides to give up for the day, and tells Daddy and the kids they can go home... Daddy wants to know if Robespierre is hired—and the director tells him, "Yes, at double the salary—on one condition." What's the condition, asks Daddy. And he's told that he and the kids must stay off the lot for the duration of the picture.

Snooks is still hollering that she wants to play in the picture—and Daddy prevails upon the director to shoot a few more feet to keep Snooks quiet... Daddy gets into the scene with Snooks, and she wants to know what she's supposed to do... Daddy tells her to bend over—she bends over... The director hollers "Camera!" Daddy proceeds to spank Snooks—Snooks cries—and the scene is over.

www.ingramcontent.com/pod-product-compliance
Lightning Source LLC
Chambersburg PA
CBHW061954180426
43198CB00036B/810